Reclaiming
the Temple Mount

"There are many entrances, there are many gates; it would be very difficult to stop a large number of people who wished to arrive at the Temple Mount from all directions. Yes, it would be very difficult to stop this. It is an idea whose time has come – the war is over the Temple Mount."

Baruch Ben Yosef, Attorney
Chairman of the Movement for Establishing the Temple
Channel 2 TV March 16, 2005

"We would like to focus attention on REVAVA - the organization has become "famous" lately, in light of multiple calls for Jews to ascend en masse to the Temple Mount... So far, the actions of REVAVA have caused harsh reactions in the Muslim sector, in Israel and in Judea and Samaria."

Yuval Rothman, Attorney
Chief Aide to the State Prosecutor
in official response of the State to Supreme Court
Jerusalem June 5, 2005

Everyone knows how fragile the situation is in this place, and therefore it is incumbent on us to act with extreme care and careful thought. Any small incident in such a place is liable to bring in its wake a big eruption, and along those lines it is possible to understand the special sensitivity of the police to prevent any incident, or threat of incident of this nature.

Supreme Court of Israel, case num. 99/76

Reclaiming

the Temple Mount

by David Ha'Ivri

HaMeir L'David המאיר לדוד

Spreading the Torah truth to hasten the redemption   הפצת תורת אמת להחשת הגאולה

www.hameir.org ׀ email: office@hameir.org ׀ Fax. 03-9366510 .פקס ׀ Tel. 03-9060875 .טל ׀ P.O.Box 4006 Ariel Israel 44837 אריאל 4006 .ת.ד ׀ 58-028546-7 .ר.ע

HaMeir L'David – Shavat 5766 (Feb. 2006)

Copyright © 2006 by David Ha'Ivri

ISBN 965-905-096-8

Printed in Israel

Published by HaMeir L'David

PO Box 960121

143 Doughty Blvd.

Inwood NY 11691

www.hameir.org

Inquiries can be made though info@hameir.org

"Situated in the center of the world,
... Jerusalem in the center of the Land of Israel,
... the sanctuary in the center of Jerusalem,
... the holy place in the center of the sanctuary,
... the ark in the center of the holy place,
... and the foundation stone before the holy place,
because from it the world was founded."

Midrash Tanchuma, Kedoshim

"By the waters of Babylon, there we sat and
wept when we remembered Zion. On the
willows there we hung up our lyres"

"If I forget thee, O Jerusalem, let my right
hand wither, let my tongue cleave to my
palate if I do not remember you, if I do not set
Jerusalem above my highest joy."

(Tehilim;137)

*"From the four corners of the earth we pray facing
Jerusalem... We pray for Jerusalem and the
restoration of the Temple service...
Building the Temple and building
the State of Israel should be the same thing..."*

Rabbi Moshe Segal

*"On Tuesday, the fourth of Heshvan, 5026, we left
Akko to ascend to Jerusalem amidst danger.
I entered into the great and holy house and
prayed there on the sixth of Cheshvan... I vowed
an oath, that I will always celebrate this day as a
personal festival, to be marked by prayer and
rejoicing in HASHEM, and by a festive meal. And
as I have merited to pray there in its ruins, so may I
and all Israel see it consoled speedily. Amen. "*

Rambam (Sefer HaCharedim)

Timeline of the First Temple

2000 BCE - Abraham journeys from Beer Sheva to Mount Moriah to offer his son Isaac to **HASHEM**.

1000 BCE - King David establishes Jerusalem as the capital of the United Kingdom of Israel.

950 BCE - King Solomon builds the First Temple on the site chosen by his father King David.

910 BCE - Kingdom is divided between Israel and Judea with Jerusalem as capital of Judea.

835 BCE – King Yoash establishes maintenance fund and repairs the Temple.

716 BCE - King Hezekiah resists Assyrian attempt to conqueror Jerusalem.

423 BCE[1] - 9th of Av - Nebuchadnezzar captures Jerusalem. The city burns and the Temple is destroyed. The inhabitants are slaughtered, and survivors are marched into captivity.

Timeline of the Second Temple

370 B.C.E. Cyrus reigns; permits Jews to return to Eretz Yisrael.

---

[1] There is a dispute among historians as to the date of the destruction of the First Temple. According to some opinions, the date is 163 years earlier, in 586 BCE.

353 B.C.E. Darius the Persian permits Jews to rebuild Temple. Despite fierce opposition of the Shomronim and other delays, an altar for sacrifice is erected on Temple Mount.

175 BCE – Hellenistic campaign of assimilation against the Jewish faith. Antiochus[2] ransacks Jerusalem, prohibits *brit milah*, study of Torah and erects an altar to Zeus in the Second Temple.

170 BCE - Jews begin the Hashmonian revolt culminating in repossession of the Temple Mount.

165 BCE - Temple purified, worship and sacrifices restored by Yehuda Macabee.

68 CE, 9th of Av, –Titus[3] besieges Jerusalem, destroys city and kills most of its inhabitants.

---

[2] Antiochus IV, Hellenistic Seleucid emperor, 175–163 BCE.
[3] Roman General Titus Flavius Vespasianus, 39–81 CE.

136 CE - Hadrian[4] constructs a pagan temple to Jupiter on the site of the Temple.

The Temple Mount In Foreign Hands

630 CE - Byzantine Christians build a shrine on the site of the Temple, which is the precursor to the Dome of the Rock.

640 CE – After conquering the Byzantine Christians, Omar Ibn-Khattab[5] refurbishes the Temple Mount, and allows Jews to build a yeshiva near it.

685-705 CE - Al-Aqsa Mosque constructed.

---

[4] Roman emperor, 117–138 CE.
[5] Caliph of Islam, 634-644 CE.

940 CE - A Karaite writer named Solomon Ben-Yerucham writes about a synagogue on the southern side of the Temple Mount.

1033 CE - Earthquake damages Al-Aqsa Mosque.

1099 CE - Violent Christian conquest of Holy Land. Many Jews and Moslems murdered. Jews sold into slavery and banished from Jerusalem. Dome of the Rock re-consecrated as "Temple Domini" and Al-Aqsa as "Temple Salomonis."

1165 CE – Rambam[6] prays on Temple Mount.

1187 CE - Saladin captures Jerusalem from Crusaders. Dome of the Rock and Al-Aqsa again Islamized.

---

[6] Rabbi Moshe ben Maimon (Maimonides) 1135 – 1204.

1556 CE - Earthquake causes considerable damage in Jerusalem.

1917 CE - Jerusalem under British military rule. Temple Mount opened to Europeans.

1927 CE – Earthquake weakens Al-Aqsa foundations.

Foreword

The Temple Mount is the only place in the world apart from Islamic and totalitarian countries where Jews are forbidden to pray.

How can a country that was established to be the "Jewish State" act in such a way? Why would a country that claims to be a democracy, discriminate against part of the population, let alone its own majority? Why won't the State of Israel protect its own people's freedom of religion? If we want Israel to be a strong sovereign country and not the vassal state that it is today, these questions regarding Israel's behavior towards the Temple Mount are vital.

Resolving this problem will immediately change the State of Israel's internal and foreign policy and allow Israel to fill its true objective and responsibility: "Tikkun Olam" and Kiddush **HASHEM**. Only then can we fulfill our purpose of being a light onto the nations.

CHAPTER ONE

FLASHBACK AT KISHLE PRISON

On the first day of the Hebrew month of Nissan in the year 5765, or April 10, 2005, I left my home in Kfar Tapuach at five o'clock in the morning. A taxi was waiting to take me for an interview on Israel's leading morning TV talk-show on Channel Two. At the same time my associate, Yisrael Meir Cohen, was being interviewed on Channel One.

That day was the climax of the first stage of our REVAVA to the Temple Mount initiative calling for thousands of Jews to enter the Temple Mount.
Channel Two also invited a leader of the Israeli Islamic movement, a movement which is involved in illegal building on the Temple Mount to set up facts on the ground to Islamize the Mount. He said that they will be bringing out thousands of Muslims to

21

"protect the mosques" from the Jews. My reply surprised him: "the mosques take up less than five percent of the area of the Temple Mount. The whole Mount is holy to the Jewish people. Why should we be banned from praying on 95% of our holy Temple Mount because you have a mosque on a tiny part of it?"

After the interview, I continued on to Jerusalem with two young men who accompanied me from Kfar Tapuach. At Jerusalem's city hall in Safra Square we met up with others, including my son Yair-Maccabee and a young man named Yonatan HaKimi.

Together we proceeded by foot toward the Jaffa Gate of the walled Old City. At the Jaffa Gate we were stopped by a very large police force that was checking every visitor, one by one. The police had set up a solid blockade, and the bomb squad was checking all bags with x-ray equipment. The police-officer in charge of the check-point asked that we accompany him to the nearby police-station (the *Kishle)* within the walls of the Old City.

Michael Ben-Chorin at the Kishle police station

At that point there were about forty people in our group, and about the same number of journalists and photographers covering the event. Meanwhile, other members of our group had already arrived at the Kotel. Many had also been detained, and many more had been unable to pass through the police barricades. None of this surprised us, because the police had closed off the Old City three days in advance to prevent entry to anyone who might be connected to our group. Inside the police station were a bunch of REVAVA activists. We were soon joined by my old friend Michael Ben-Chorin and three of his teenaged daughters, all wearing "REVAVA to The Temple Mount" T-shirts.

It was Michael and his wife Ariela who had introduced me to my wife Molly some years ago. Held up at the Kishle police station, it brought back memories of an event seventeen years earlier, when I was detained in this same police station for other activities involving the Temple Mount.

25

It was 1988, only a few months after being married, when I was arrested for going up to the Temple Mount with a group of fellow students. I had been ascending the Mount regularly, and my wife had expressed concern that something might happen to me or that I might be arrested. As a newly and happily married young man, I wasn't sure what to do, so I asked my rabbi for advice. Rabbi Meir Kahane said to me, "David, listen. You have to respect your wife and be considerate of her feelings, but there are things that have to be done for the Jewish people and if this has to be done, then you have to put personal issues aside." I took the Rabbi's advice and continued my trips to the Temple Mount.

During those days, we were among the very few Torah-observant Jews who would ascend the Temple Mount regularly. We often stayed over at the yeshiva for Shabbat, and following our morning prayers and festive meal, we would walk as a group from the yeshiva building in Jerusalem's Mekor Baruch neighborhood. It was about a twenty-minute walk to the Old City, through Sha'ar Shechem - the Damascus Gate, and through the Arab market to the entrance of the Temple Mount near the western wall. On this day, May 28, 1988, we were a group of fifteen yeshiva students attempting to enter the Temple Mount and pray with a minyan, a quorum of ten Jews.

At that time, Jews were permitted by the police to enter the Temple Mount only through the Mugrabim gate, which stands just above the Kotel to the right. We ascended the ramp that leads up to the large green Mugrabim Gate, and awaited entry to the Temple Mount. Standing in our way were two Israeli policemen taking down detailed personal information, ID numbers, and names of any Jews who requested entry. They allowed only a few to enter each time, spoiling our plans to ascend with a minyan.

We tried to persuade them that they must allow at least ten Jews in at a time, so we could pray properly. When that didn't work, we attempted to push ourselves in. Of the two policemen, one was an Arab. Also present were members of the Waqf (the Islamic custodians), refusing to let us through.

Israeli Police at Mugrabi gate

The Waqf members began hitting us with their big walkie-talkies, and a fight ensued. Arabs started streaming out of the mosque with steel bars. Being greatly outnumbered (and unarmed), we had no choice but to slowly retreat down the ramp.

My friend Benzi Gopstein and I were arrested at the bottom of the ramp and charged with assaulting police officers. The Israeli police officers claimed that we had hit them and assaulted the Waqf. In truth, we had been merely defending ourselves from their attack. We had been simply trying to pray on the Temple Mount. Benzi and I spent that summer in jail. The time was not wasted, as we studied Torah and learned more about the history of the Mount, preparing ourselves for the day when we would reclaim it for our people.

David Ha'Ivri

CHAPTER TWO

CENTRALITY OF THE MOUNT

Rebuilding the Temple on its chosen spot, the Temple Mount, and restoring the worship of **HASHEM** there is the central aspiration of the Jewish people.

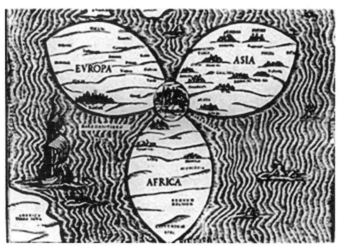

"Jerusalem, Center of the World",
from: H. Buenting, Itinerarium Sacrae Scripturae, 1581

In each of the three daily prayers – evening, morning, and afternoon – and in the birkat ha'Mazon blessing after meals, we pray to return to Zion and to rebuild the Temple. Some Jews awaken at midnight to mourn for the Temple, sitting on the floor and reading Psalms by candlelight.

Also called "Mount Moriah," the Temple Mount in Jerusalem is the historic location of the Holy Temple, a place of the highest historical and religious significance. Our sages teach that the first man, Adam, was created from the earth of this location. Abraham our father followed **HASHEM**'s direction to this location to bind his son Isaac as an offering to **HASHEM**. Our father Jacob laid down to rest in Bet El and dreamt that he saw a ladder ascending from that same spot up to the heavens with angels climbing up and down.

Some nine centuries later King David[7] purchased the area from Aravnah the Yevusite, and erected an altar for sacrifice. Although the Yevusi offered it as a gift, David insisted on paying for it:

And the king said unto Aravnah; No, but I will surely buy it from thee at a price; neither will I offer burnt offerings unto the Lord my God of that which doth cost me nothing. So David bought the oxen and the threshing floor for fifty shekels of silver.[8]

A generation later his son, King Solomon, erected the Temple there. The building of the Temple in Jerusalem brought into being a new law for the people of Israel: from here-after sacrifices could be offered only at the Temple and no longer allowed outside of Jerusalem. Three pilgrimages - Passover, Shavuot, and Sukkot brought the

---

[7] King of Israel, 1004-965 BCE.
[8] II Samuel 24: 24.

gathering of the majority of the nation to this site. With ritual worship concentrated in Jerusalem, the city's population was swollen enormously during these three times yearly. The huge assembly during the pilgrimage periods made Jerusalem an important trade and commercial center.

For four hundred and ten years the Temple stood as the national and spiritual center of the Jewish people until it was destroyed by the Babylonians, who slaughtered a great number of Jews and marched the survivors away in chains to Babylon. In the words of the Psalmist; "*By the rivers of Babylon there we sat down, yea we wept when we remembered Zion*".[9]

After seventy years of exile in Babylon, the first Jewish pioneers began to return to the Land of Israel, but only a generation later could they

---

[9] Psalms 137:1.

continue the task of building the Second Temple. Ezra and Nehemiah brought the people back to the land of Israel and reinstated the *avodah*, the ritual of the Temple. Despite fierce opposition of the Shomronim and other delays, the Second Temple was eventually built in 353 BCE.

Nehemiah undertook a major project of rebuilding the walls and fortifying the city as part of his program to reinstate Jerusalem as a national capital. He required every family in the land of Judah to send ten of its members to live in Jerusalem.

In the fourth century BCE, Alexander the Great[10] conquered the entire region along with Jerusalem. His empire was eventually split into three kingdoms, each ruled by one of his generals. Jerusalem came under the rule of the Greek Hellenistic Seleucid Syrians. As their Hellenist culture became increasingly popular amongst Jews, tension grew between them and the traditionalist Torah observing Jews. When Antiochus[11] enacted religious decrees directly affecting the Temple ritual worship such as mandatory idolatry inside the Temple, Torah loyal Jews were infuriated.

In 168 BCE the Hasmonean revolt broke out, led by Yehuda HaMaccabee. During his leadership, the

---

[10] Alexander III King of Macedonia, 356-323 BCE.
[11] Antiochus IV Ruler of the Seleucid Empire, 215-163 BCE.

Temple Mount was liberated from the Greeks and Hellenists, and the Temple was purified and restored as the Jewish spiritual center. Some 20 afterwards, Simeon the Maccabee defeated the Greek-Hellenistic Jews entirely, ushering in an 80 year period of Jewish political independence in Jerusalem. For the first time since the period of the Second Temple had begun, Jews had finally achieved complete national independence in the Land of Israel.

Due to corruption and infighting among heirs, four decades of Hasmonean Dynasty came to an end, and they were removed from power by the Roman Republic, who appointed Herod as King of Judea in 40 BC.

Following Herod's death, Roman oppression and Jewish resistance intensified. Toward the end of the 1st century BCE, a revolt broke out. On the ninth day of the Hebrew month of Av, in 68 CE,

Jerusalem fell to the Roman legions under the command of Titus. The Romans destroyed what had been a flourishing city. Jerusalem's buildings were burnt and its Jewish inhabitants exiled. The Second Temple, which had stood for 420 years, was destroyed. The Temple's significance as the foundation of the state and its religious life, and as the stronghold and symbol of national spirit and faith - this more than anything else brought on Titus' order to burn it down.

Since that time, the people of Israel, dispersed in the exile to the four corners of the earth, have prayed daily to return to Zion and rebuild the holy Temple. A story relates that Napolean Bonaparte once entered a synagogue on Tish B'Av, the solemn fast day observed each year that marks the anniversary of the Holy Temple's destruction. Seeing the Jewish mourners seated on the floor crying, he asked what terrible disaster had befallen them. He was told: "The Jews are in mourning for their Temple, Your Excellency". Upon learning that the Jews were grieving over the destruction of the Temple in Jerusalem more than 1700 years earlier, the emperor remarked: "Such a people will never be destroyed. If they still remember to mourn for their Temple of so long ago, they will surely see it rebuilt."

In our 2,000 year old exile, the importance and holiness of the Temple Mount has never lessened. Reclaiming the Mount and rebuilding the Temple have always been a major concern of great thinkers and movers of the Jewish people.

Rabbi Moshe Segal was a pioneer and a founder of Kfar Chabad, who moved on to resettle the Jewish Quarter of Jerusalem after the Six Day War in June, 1967. He was also a founder of the Temple Mount faithful movement. He wrote:

What is Judaism without the Temple Mount? We fool ourselves into believing that Jerusalem is being rebuilt: Behold! The city is full of places of Torah study. But something is missing! As long as the site of the

Rabbi Moshe Segal

Temple is captive and held by Goyim, Judaism has in no way reached its goal. The pinnacle of the Nation of Israel is the Temple Mount. "The Lord will reign forever and ever" – the purpose of the Nation of Israel is to enthrone GOD in His world. When Israel is sovereign, GOD is sovereign. When Israel lacks sovereignty, the Divine is degraded.

The values symbolized by a rebuilt Jerusalem and the Temple Mount are not only religious. One doesn't have to be a rabbi to understand that without our historical connection to Jerusalem, without this link to the past, without the continuity with the ancient kingdoms of Israel for whom the Temple was the national center, we become no better then foreign invaders in the land. One does not have to be a Torah scholar to understand that giving up Israel's past means giving up its future as well. That is why even un-observant Jewish nationalists who fought the British occupation, viewed the Temple as an essential national goal.

One of the greatest of these fighters was Yair (Avraham) Stern. A Jewish national poet and revolutionary, Stern was a visionary and founder of the "LEHI" - Freedom Fighters for Israel. Though murdered by the British on February 12, 1942, his ideology was the inspiration for the eventual expulsion of the British occupying forces from Palestine in the pre-state days of Israel. He drew up the "18 Principles For the Rebirth Of the Nation," in which he closes: *"To Rebuild the Temple as a symbol of the age of the redemption of the Jewish people."*

As secularized as the state of Israel is today, its people instinctively understand the importance of the Temple Mount. The results of a survey in late 1995 by the Guttman Institute of Applied Social Research, indicate how important the Temple Mount is to Israeli Jews. 84% of the total sample, of which 73% is non-observant, say it is important that Jews be able to pray on the Temple Mount.

But that is not the case. This minimal right to pray on the holiest site of Judaism has been taken from us, and it is therefore incumbent upon us to reclaim the Temple Mount.

CHAPTER THREE

A GOLDEN COVER UP

Atop the Temple Mount today there is no Temple, but rather huge Arab structures. One of these is the **Al-Aqsa mosque**, which is part of a complex of buildings that stand on the southern side of the Temple Mount. The other is the Dome of the Rock which stands in the very center of the Mount, and due to its visibility, is probably considered by most people to be the most identifiable symbol of Jerusalem.

Who built these structures and for what purpose? Why was this site chosen to build Islamic shrines? Answers to these questions shed light on the true importance of Jerusalem and the Temple Mount to the Muslims.

In the year 636 CE, the Christian Byzantine[12] period came to an end following the Battle of Yarmuk.[13] The victorious Muslims made for Jerusalem and laid siege to the city for two years. After eighteen months the besieging army was joined by a second force, led by Ben-Jarah, and finally the city was captured from the Christian Byzantine Empire.

According to Muslim tradition, Ben-Jarah called on Omar to assume the crown of victory over Jerusalem, which had been an important Christian (and of course, Jewish) city. A mosque on the Temple Mount was built on the southern side of the Mount – which today is known as Al-Aqsa. **The southern side was specifically chosen in order that the Moslem worshippers would face only**

---

[12] **Byzantine Empire** is the term conventionally used to describe the Greek-speaking Roman Empire during the Middle Ages.
[13] The **Battle of Yarmuk** took place between the Muslim Arabs and the Byzantine Empire resulting in Muslim takeover of Syria.

Mecca, and not the Holy of Holies of the Temple, during prayer.

Al-Aqsa Mosque in the nineteenth century

While it is not clear precisely when the Al-Aqsa mosque was built, radiocarbon dating of wooden beams and panels removed from the building during renovations in the 1930's show that the material used dates as far back as the 9th century BCE, hundreds of years before the Muslims conquered Jerusalem. Much of the material was analyzed as derived from cedar of Lebanon and

Cyprus, and is likely to be the same material which was used to build the Holy Temple.

If the Al-Aqsa mosque presents a problem to Jews focused on the dream of rebuilding the Temple, all the more so regarding the Dome of the Rock - the other large structure that stands on the Mount. This massive golden domed structure stands directly over where the Holy of Holies of the Temple stood. What is its true significance to Islam? What is its history?

Muslims praying with their backs to the Dome of the Rock

The **Dome of the Rock** was built around the year 630 CE, and is sometimes called the mosque of Omar, even though it is not really a mosque. Because it is located on the highest plateau in the center of the Temple Mount, it has become Jerusalem's best known landmark.

According to Muslim tradition, it was from this spot that Muhammad ascended through the heavens on his flying horse ("El Buraque"), after his ride from Mecca to Jerusalem. It is this magic ride by Mohammad which constitutes the earliest Muslim spiritual connection to the Mount and the source of the Temple Mount's significance to Islam.

But a closer look reveals that this entire story connecting Muhammad to the Temple Mount is a "reach," based on a single verse in the Koran which says: "Glory be to Him, who carried His servant by night from the Holy Mosque (in Mecca) to the **further mosque**, the precincts of which we have blessed."

This expression, "the further mosque", was later extrapolated by Islam commentators to indicate the Al-Aqsa mosque on the Temple Mount, and from there the tradition evolved. But the fact is, not only isn't the Temple Mount mentioned in the Koran, but neither is Jerusalem! There was not even a mosque on the Temple Mount during Mohammad's time. Jerusalem was controlled by Byzantine Christians until 636, four years after Mohammad's death in 632.

While the Moslem significance of the Mount is dubious according to its own religious sources, a look at the historical and political context in which The Dome of the Rock was built casts even greater doubt on the Moslem claim. The fact is, it is not clear at all if the Dome of the Rock was originally built where it was because of any religious significance. There are well-substantiated theories which hold that it was built on an already existing church.

For centuries before the Muslim conquest, Jerusalem was controlled by Byzantine Christians. During their rule, Persians, who were aided by Jews who jumped at the chance to end centuries of religious persecution at the hands of the Christians, managed briefly to capture the city between 614

and 628. Some say that the Jews took this as a sign of the beginning of the redemption, as it was the Persian king Cyrus who had given permission to build the Second Temple and end the Babylonian

The Dome of the Rock in 1927, before it was gold-plated

49

Exile. Many Jews thought that the end of Christian rule over Jerusalem was a sign that the redemption was near, and that the Third Temple would shortly be built.

But when the Byzantine Christians retook control of the city in 628, they did not take kindly to the fact that Jews had aided the Persians in the conquest of their city. To show that they were here to stay, they built a church on the site of the Holy Temple, an octagonal structure **that was the precursor to the current Dome of the Rock.** Jews were banned from approaching the site and even from praying publicly in Jerusalem.

According to other opinions, a church had *already* existed on the site, was burned down when the Persians took the city, and was then rebuilt by the Byzantine Christians later. The fact that the Dome of the Rock today resembles a modified Byzantine

Church sheds light on the various architectural oddities found there.

The Dome does not resemble any style of mosque architecture, but is virtually identical to a typical octagonal Byzantine church of the period. It bears particular resemblance to the Church of the Holy Sepulture in the Old City and churches on the Mount of Olives. The building does not face Mecca as all mosques must, and lacks the traditional "qibla" wall which shows the direction of Mecca, to which all Moslems must face while praying. It should not come as a surprise that to this day, the Dome of the Rock has never been used as a mosque or even a site of prayer.

Through the course of Islamic history, Muslims have always "converted" places holy to others, to Islam. The Dome of the Rock was Islamized due to "political considerations." Moslems have always taken religious interest in Jerusalem when it served practical interests, or made a statement. First and foremost it was done as an affront to the Jews and even more so to the Christians, as a steady reminder that the Muslims are now in control of Jerusalem, and that Islam is the superior religion. This pattern has recurred at least five times over 14 centuries. It was done in Pagan times, and as mentioned a Church was built on the Holy of Holies by the Byzantine Christians as an affront to the Jews. Later, during the Crusades, the building was once again converted into a church until Saladin captured Jerusalem and once again converted it back to a Muslim site.

Arab kids playing soccer on the Temple Mount

The point is that Jerusalem never was a distinctly holy place for Moslems. It is not once mentioned in the Koran, and outside of Muhamad's afore-mentioned "dream ride" in Islamic tradition, there is no historical evidence that Mohammed ever visited the city. Nor has Jerusalem ever served as an Islamic cultural center. That has always been the function of Mecca, which is the "Jerusalem" of

Islam. That is the place where Moslems believe that Abraham nearly sacrificed Ishmael (instead of the Jewish belief that it was Isaac who was nearly sacrificed, not in Mecca, but on the Temple Mount). Mohammed lived most of his life in Mecca and there all of the key events of the Koran took place. Mecca is the direction in which Moslems pray five times each day, and do not permit non-Moslems to set foot.

Via the presence of these shrines (Al-Aqsa and the Dome of the Rock) on the Temple Mount, the Arabs set up facts on the ground to deny Jewish connection to the site. Although today's Islamic Waqf officials deny any historical Jewish link to the Temple Mount, a 1930 booklet about the site published by the supreme Moslem body in Jerusalem at the time states very clearly that the site's identification with the First Temple is **"beyond dispute"**.

The nine-page English-language tourist guide, entitled "A Brief Guide to *Al-Haram Al-Sharif*" states:

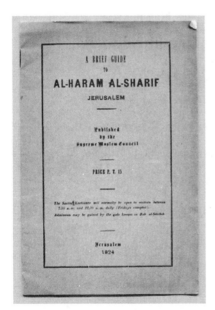

*The site is one of the oldest in the world. Its sanctity dates from the earliest times. **Its identity with the site of Solomon's Temple is beyond dispute**. This, too, is the spot, according to universal belief, on which David built an altar unto the Lord, and offered burnt offerings and peace offerings."* A footnote refers the reader to the Tanach, book of Samuel II 24:25.

While the booklet obviously focuses on the Moslem connection to the site, we see that the authors make no effort to deny its Jewish roots as the Muslims do today.

Whether the Dome of the Rock was built from a Byzantine Church or not, **its location was chosen strictly as an acknowledgement of the holiness of the historic location of the Temple**. Over the years, with the radicalization of Islamic imperialism, history has been rewritten, and these structures have become tools for the **denial** of history - a massive golden cover up of the true Jewish national heritage.

CHAPTER FOUR

JUNE 1967

IS THE TEMPLE MOUNT

IN OUR HANDS?

An Israeli personal-carrier on the way to the Lions gate

June 1948 CE - Declaration of the State of Israel with Jerusalem as its capital city.

1951 CE - Jordan's King Abdullah assassinated by Arabs on Temple Mount.

June, 1967 CE - Old City captured by Israel. Israeli flag flies temporarily over the Temple Mount.

Rabbi Goren celebrating victory with soldiers

We recite in the Musaf prayer, "*because of our sins, we have been exiled from the land.*" As a result of a 2000 year exile we had been distanced from the Temple Mount and unable to conduct the rituals as obligated by the Torah. When the Jewish people finally began to return to their land, they found the Temple Mount controlled by foreigners who denied them access. Its boundary, the Western Wall, was all that remained for Jews to pray to.

In the 1967 Six Day War, all that changed, and the Temple Mount finally became ours again. Through a series of miracles not witnessed since the days of the Macabees, not only did the Temple Mount fall into our hands, but so did the Sinai Peninsula, the Golan Heights, Judea and Samaria.

 The events were as follows. Fretful of impending invasion, Israel carried out a pre-emptive strike on Egyptian forces in the Sinai, destroying the entire Egyptian air force while its planes were still on the ground. Furthermore, Israeli troops took over the "West Bank," the Gaza strip, and the Golan

Heights as well as capturing the Sinai Peninsula all the way to the Suez Canal which is the natural border between the land of Israel and the African continent.

This conquest more then doubled the size of the State of Israel. By the end of the second day of the brief but bloody war, Israeli paratroopers had broken though the Lion's gate entering the Arab occupied old city of Jerusalem to capture the treasured Temple Mount from Jordan. Shortly afterward the Israeli flag rose over the Dome of the Rock.

Colonel Motta Gur radioed to the Israeli headquarters proclaiming *"The Temple Mount is in our hands"*. Jews were once again in control of the site of Solomon's Temple in what was a striking fulfillment of Biblical prophesy. For believing Jews, the hope for the construction of the Third Temple and the redemption of Israel was now closer then ever before.

Only days after the Temple Mount was liberated by the IDF, General Rabbi Shlomo Goren, Chief Rabbi of Israel's army, had the military surveyors measure the area of the Temple Mount. In vacant buildings  on the Mount he established a yeshiva called the IDF Rabbinical College and began announcing the call for Jews to ascend. He placed advertisements in the Israeli newspapers calling upon Jews to come to prayer on the Temple Mount on Tisha B'Av, only a few weeks after the Temple Mount was liberated.

In an interview, General Uzi Narkiss reported that on June 7, 1967, a few hours after East Jerusalem fell into Israeli hands, Rabbi Shlomo Goren told him "now is the time to put 100 kilograms of explosives into the Mosque of Omar so that we may rid ourselves of it once and for all." His request was denied. According to Goren's aide Menahem Hacohen, he had not suggested blowing up the mosque, but had merely stated that "if, during the course of the war a bomb had fallen on the mosque and it would have - you know - disappeared - that would have been a good thing." But later that year in a speech to a military convention, Rabbi Goren spoke words that seem to verify the former version: "Certainly we should have blown it up. It is a tragedy for generations that we did not do so. ... I myself would have gone up there and wiped it off the ground completely so that there would be no trace that a Mosque of Omar was ever up there."[14]

---

[14] Hilary Appelman, Associated Press, 31 December 1997.

The Israeli politicians became very uneasy about Rabbi Goren's activities of bringing Jews to the Temple Mount, bringing up a Torah scroll, studying there and gathering minyanim for regular prayer sessions. As a result, a ruling was made forbidding Rabbi Goren from any further activity on the Mount, forcing him to abandon his call for mass prayers, and to abort his plans for a military rabbinical college-yeshiva on the Mount.

To top it off, in an incredible display of lack of faith, the Israeli government returned the gift that GOD had given us. Moshe Dayan assembled the Waqf caretakers, and gave them the keys to the gates of the Temple Mount, relinquishing the very short-lived Jewish control.

Rabbi Shlomo Goren on the Temple Mount

The tragedy is that until that time, the Muslims themselves had believed that they were only taking care of the Temple Mount until the day would come when it would return to its rightful owners, the Jews. But when that day came, and they saw the weakness of Israeli authority, its refusal to take charge, and its general disdain for the Mount, the Muslim confidence and aspirations grew.

Unfortunately, as long as the government of Israel is run by people who are far from Torah Judaism, there is a real concern that the situation will not change for the better. They, like the Muslims, see a liberated Temple as a threat to the continuation of their power. They understand that a state with Jewish national pride is the alternative to their hellenistic rule. The gross act of weakness of giving the keys to the Muslim Waqf symbolizes Israeli government mindset in a nutshell. Giving autonomy to the Arabs on the Temple Mount serves as the model of Israeli policy concerning *all* issues on the national agenda. In the words of the poet Uri Tzvi Greenberg:[15] *"He who controls the Temple Mount, controls Jerusalem. And he who controls Jerusalem, controls the land of Israel."* And he who forfeits control of the Mount, loses control of the land.

---

[15] Considered a foremost Hebrew poet of his generation, Greenberg used his poetry to espouse a religious mystical view of Zionism and to further Revisionism's Jewish nationalism.

By abandoning our claim to the Temple Mount we are abandoning the most basic of our claims to the land of Israel.

CHAPTER FIVE

WILL IT BLOW?

In December, 2003, a conference was held in Herzliya discussing the issue of the State of Israel versus terror. The head of the Shin Bet[16] at the time, Avi Dichter, spoke in detail of "a threat of Jewish terrorism." Hezi Kallo,

The Dome of the Rock

who in the mid-1990s headed the Shin Bet's branch for non-Arab affairs, (another way of saying "Jewish affairs") explained afterwards to the media, that Dichter was referring to the possibility of a Jewish strike on the Temple Mount.

---

[16] The **Shabak** is an acronym of "Sherut ha-Bitahon ha-Klali" (General Security Service) AKA the Shin Bet.

Kallo believes that "a Jewish strike at the Temple Mount, in an effort to torpedo a political process" is a possibility that definitely has to be taken into account. He says that a potential threat exists, but it is difficult to know from where.

Carmi Gillon, who headed Israel's Shin Bet from 1994 to 1996, is also concerned about an attack on the Temple Mount:

Alongside ideological criminals [sic.] capable of deep and serious political messianic thinking like Jewish underground leader Yehuda Etzion, we have witnessed additional varieties of criminal [sic.] ideological activity over the Temple Mount.
Rabbi Meir Kahane, leader of the Kach movement, was placed under administrative detention in 1980 because he intended to fire a missile at the Temple Mount. Eccentric messianic groups of criminal born-

again Jews [sic.] also sought to assist the coming of the messiah by blowing up the Dome of the Rock. These included the messianic Lifta gang that was arrested in 1984 and the TNT gang arrested a year earlier.

Others keep the Temple Mount cause on the back burner. They consider the abandonment of this perfect symbol of the Greater Land of Israel to strangers and the ban on Jewish prayer rights on the Mount as an open wound at the heart of the land. They are represented by the Temple Mount Faithful, headed by Gershon Solomon, which makes do with intensive protests, albeit within the limits of the law.

The radicalization process over the Temple Mount continues. What, then, is the "red line" which, once crossed, will bring matters to a head? I assess that this will be the dismantling of settlements. When the

Yamit settlements were removed from Sinai in 1982 we were not far from an attack on the Mount.

The major fear and paranoia which grips the Israeli authorities over an attack on the mosques, is not an ethical concern for Arab holy sites, but rather the reaction of the Arab world if such an attack took place. They are convinced that it would lead to JIHAD - an all out war by the Arabs to wipe out the State of Israel and a total destabilization of the region.

An examination of the facts shows how this line of thinking reflects the exile mentality of the Israeli establishment. Since 1967, a number of attempts have been made by individuals to attack the mosques or the Muslims on the Temple Mount. But despite all of the threats and declarations by the Arabs (which we hear **anyway** on a continual basis since the establishment of the State of Israel), they have not launched World War III.

In 1969, two years after the Temple Mount was liberated by the Israeli Defense Forces and subsequently handed over to the Muslim Waqf, the Al-Aqsa Mosque was targeted. Dennis Michael Rohan, an Australian tourist who had come to Israel to study Hebrew and work on a kibbutz, entered the Al-Aqsa Mosque before normal visiting hours and set fire to the mosque.

Israeli firefighters and sixteen fire trucks labored for hours to put out the fire. Muslims still accused the Jews of arson, claiming that the Israeli firefighters sprayed gasoline on the fire and cut off the water supply to ensure the mosque's destruction. When Rohan was arrested and identified as a Christian fundamentalist and a foreigner, it made little difference. Muslims called for a general strike, and

Arab leaders called for a holy war against Israel, which obviously did not happen.

After the Rohan affair, Shabtai Ben-Dov[17] wrote:

*Even when the rumor that the "last mosque" (Al-Aqsa) had been torched in order to give way to the Temple, nothing out of the ordinary happened, either in the Muslim world or among the Muslims in Jerusalem itself. Even if it really transpired, and we had taken away the Temple Mount mosques and replaced them with the Temple, there would have been no practical background for the Islamic world to have aroused itself to launch any kind of Jihad, to storm us seriously, or even harm us in some other manner much more efficient and significant than that with which it tries to hurt us **anyway**. It therefore seems that even if we were to rise up and carry out this "terrible act", nothing would really*

---

[17] Shabtai Ben-Dov - Jewish revolutionary, philosopher and Lehi ideologue who sought to restore the kingdom of Israel.

happen to us here and the Muslim world would quickly adjust to the new situation.

In April 11, 1982, Allen Goodman, an American born immigrant who became an Israeli soldier, went on a shooting rampage on the Temple Mount. Storming into the Al Aqsa Mosque with an M-16 rifle, Goodman killed a Waqf guard and wounded other Arabs. The incident set off Arab rioting and strikes that ended within a week. He was convicted a year later and sentenced to life plus two terms of twenty years.

In March 1983, several dozen Yeshiva students were arrested by the Israeli police after a Waqf member complained that he heard digging beneath the Temple Mount. Equipped with arms, shovels, and diagrams of the

Rabbi Yisrael Ariel

73

underground passageways leading to the area, the group planned to "settle" the Temple Mount. Taking a page out of the book of the settlement movement, their goal was to set up facts on the ground and "squat" in the underground chambers in the area of the Solomon's Stables on the south side of the Mount. Most of those arrested in connection with the incident were discovered in the home of Rabbi Yisrael Ariel, head of the "Temple Institute," an organization we will discuss later. A decade later, the Arabs set up their own facts on the ground by taking over these same Solomon Stables and Islamizing them, as we will see in Chapter 7.

In early 1984, the Shabak arrested what they called "the Jewish Underground", a group of settlers who were accused of attacks against Arabs in Judea and Samaria. Members of this group had also planned to blow up the Dome of the Rock.

This coincided with the time that the Israeli government under Prime Minster Menachem Begin was in the process of giving away the Sinai to the Egyptians.

Yehuda Etzion

Members of the "Jewish Underground" believed that an attack on the Temple Mount would disrupt the peace process and stop the withdrawal from the Sinai and even hasten the Redemption. Such a move, they felt, can usher in the coming of the Messiah. The group's leader, Yehuda Etzion[18], teamed up with fellow revolutionary, Kabalist[19] Yeshua Ben-Shushan, an officer in the IDF at the time. Ben-Shushan believed the Temple Mount was emitting a beam of spiritual energy which was harnessed by whatever shrine was built upon it. A Jewish mystic, he held that the

---

[18] Yehuda Etzion, a leading activist for the Temple Mount.
[19] Scholar of Kabbalah, the hidden Torah of mysticism.

75

physical act of removing the mosques would have strong spiritual implications.

Etzion felt that their operation on the Temple Mount could potentially trigger the transformation of the state of Israel from one system of laws to another, from the nation of Israel to the Kingdom of Israel. They held that as long as the Dome of the Rock stood in place of the Holy Temple, the redemption for Israel would be delayed. Both consulted with rabbis whose names were never publicized.

Their plan was to scale the Temple Mount walls from outside the Old City and plant 28 explosives at specially targeted locations. By the beginning of 1984, Etzion's plans to demolish the Dome of the Rock were in its final stages, and the group had begun practicing timed assaults on a scale model in the deserts south of Jerusalem. But on April 27, 1984, the entire conspiracy was exposed when members of the group were caught by the Shabak "red-handed" while engaged in another activity of planting bombs on Arab busses in Jerusalem. The bombs were defused and the arrests that followed ended the career of the most daring Jewish terror underground in nearly forty years. In the ensuing trial, Yehuda Etzion claimed he had to destroy the Muslim mosque on the Temple Mount because the Israeli government refused to "purify the area" themselves.

In a unique publication, *"Har HaBayit"*, published while in jail, Etzion explained how the Temple Mount operation fits into the general theory of Redemption:

The expurgation of Temple Mount will prepare the hearts for the understanding and further advancing of our full Redemption. The purified Mount shall be—if God wishes—the ground and the anvil for the future process of promoting the next holy elevation.[20]

In an interview to Israeli Army Radio he said: *"The Dome of the Rock is the wrong structure in the wrong place at the wrong time, because it is right and proper that our Third Temple should stand there."*

More recently, during the Gaza pullout by the Israeli government under P.M. Sharon in 2005, Etzion added that the act of attacking the mosques is a proper one in its own right, and not just as a tactic to thwart the withdrawal plan. *"In order to build the Third Temple we need to remove the Dome of the Rock. That is an endeavor that is not only worthy, but essential, and which will produce a revolution in values and culture."*

---

[20] Yehuda Etzion, *Har HaBayi,* (Jerusalem, 1985).

He does not believe that razing the Dome of the Rock will lead to an all out war with the Arab world: *"If Israel shows determination and not weakness, the message will be received in the entire world. I don't envision any missiles flying in our direction. We're not talking about a terrible act, but a necessary act. Today there are a handful of believers, but if the desire for a complete revolution filters down into the general public - there may not be any need for the act to be committed by fringe groups, but as an act of the state. That is what I hope for."*

Around the same time that the members of the "Jewish Underground" were apprehended, another group called "Lifta" had similar plans. The Lifta group was a group of Baali Tshuva[21], who began

---

[21] Secular Jews who become religious.

observing Torah and studying Kabbala[22]. The name Lifta is derived from an abandoned Arab village in Jerusalem, where members of the group lived. They too believed that blowing up the mosques on the Temple Mount would quicken the Redemption. Some of the members of the Lifta group were people who had ties with criminal figures and through those contacts were able to acquire explosives. They actually came close to carrying out their plans. On January 26, 1984 at about 10 PM, members of the Lifta group climbed over the eastern wall of the Temple Mount with their knapsack full of explosives and started scouting out the area. While

Weapons confiscated from the Lifta group in 1984

they were walking around on the Mount they bumped into one of the Muslim Waqf caretakers. It is hard to say who was more surprised. Both parties

---

[22] Mysticism.

turned around and ran the other way. Apparently the Lifta members were so stunned, they dropped their bundles of explosives and ran back to the eastern wall, climbed down their ladders and ropes, got into their beat-up old van and drove back to Lifta. The Waqf called the police and showed them the knapsack full of explosives that had been deserted.

The police examined the packages and dismantled the explosives, but still had no idea who had infiltrated the Temple Mount.

Only months later, after following leads from various common criminals who "helped" the police in order to receive reduced sentences on various petty crimes, the Lifta group was exposed and apprehended. Shimon Barda, its leader, was imprisoned for a number of years for planning and almost blowing-up the Dome of the Rock.

Israeli authorities are continually concerned about what they call a possible mega-terror attack on the Temple Mount. According to Yoel Lerner, who served time in prison during the 1970's and 1980's because of plans to strike at the Temple Mount mosques, individuals may possibly try to reconstruct his plan. "It happened once or twice; there is no reason it won't happen again," he says. Lerner also offers a more specific evaluation: "As long as there are some `hilltop' youth around here who consider Nati Ozeri[23] a paragon of virtue, anything is possible."

Lerner adds that he knew Ozeri and says: "He was one of these young people who are capable of taking action concerning the Temple Mount, if someone were to point him in the right direction. He

---

[23] Netanel Ozeri, 34, a leader of the "hilltop movement", was murdered in January 2003 by Arabs.

could reach conclusions similar to the ones I reached in 1974, during the period of the evacuation of parts of Sinai."[24]

The above attempts to remove the mosques or to physically "conquer" the Mount from the Moslems display the ultimate self-sacrifice. They are attempts to purify the impure, to put an end to atrocious Chillul Hashem. For simply changing the "status-quo" on the Mount, or succeeding in having the Waqf "allow" us to pray, or even building a small "shul" is not enough. A sanctification of God's Name cannot be achieved through a desecration of it. For the very fact that we must ask the Arabs permission, is **in itself** a Chillul Hashem. The very fact that that the Arabs rule there and control our destiny on the Mount, is a Chillul Hashem.

---

[24] Nadav Shragai – Haaretz newspaper April, 7 2004.

David Ha'Ivri

CHAPTER SIX

DON'T MOVE YOUR LIPS; WE ARE WATCHING YOU

Can you picture policemen on the job monitoring people's lips to see if they are praying? Well, this is routine procedure on Israel's Temple Mount. Jews who wish to pray on the Temple Mount are routinely arrested for "provoking" Arabs.

A Jewish woman was even arrested for simply closing her eyes on the Temple Mount. After sitting down on a bench and closing her eyes, she was accosted by the Waqf and interrogated. When she told them that she is a student at Hebrew University studying the Second Temple period, they responded: "You really believe there was a Second Temple? You plan to destroy the Dome [of the

Rock] and build the Second Temple!" The Waqf officials then turned her over to the Israel police, where she was held and questioned for four hours. During the questioning, a police officer told her that she was being charged with the crime of "praying on the Temple Mount".[25]

Any Jew who gives an impression that the Temple Mount is holy to him, will find himself under police surveillance. One day in January 2005, while visiting the Temple with my friends, Matthew and Julia Wohl, I was pointing out certain landmarks and discussing various theories concerning the exact area where the Temple, its buildings and courtyards stood. As we walked, I noticed a man in civilian clothes following us. My first thought was that he was a plain-clothes policeman.

As we continued our walk, this man caught up to us

---

[25] Israel National Radio - Arutz 7 Nov. 1999.

and broke into our conversation. He said that from what he overheard, I seemed to be knowledgeable on the subject of the Temple Mount.

I replied that I know a few things about the subject. "And what about you – what do you do?" I asked. "Oh, I'm just here," he responded. "Are you a cop?" I asked. After some hemming and hawing, he stated unconvincingly that he was a student of archaeology who was researching the Temple Mount. I decided to call his bluff by asking him his theory as to where the Temple stood. The nonsense he answered made it clear that he was totally ignorant of anything concerning the Temple, its history and archaeology. At that point I heard voices emitting from a radio he had concealed under his shirt. When I asked for his name, he said, "Ploni Almoni", which is the Hebrew equivalent for "John Doe." He continued trying to draw me back into conversation with him. As we exited the gate of the Mount, this undercover cop went and joined his uniformed friends.

Jews followed by police on the Temple Mount

There have been other incidents where police officers equipped with small video cameras followed me. Once I was asked by them: "When will we get rid of these Muslim dogs?" I refrained from answering. It was obvious that they were trying to entrap and incriminate me on film in order to have an excuse to ban me from visiting the Mount.

Indeed, a walk on the Temple Mount can be a downright humiliating experience for a Jew.

Dr. Michael Gelfand is the president of an influential synagogue in Palm Beach. On one of his visits to Jerusalem, I offered to accompany him on a visit to the Temple Mount. At 9AM we met at the police check-post on the way up to Mugrabim Gate, next to the Kotel, and started our way up the ramp to Mugrabim Gate. Being experienced with the procedure Jews are required to go through before entering the Mount, I am already used to the intensive "security" checks. But I must say that I was embarrassed for the State of Israel for making a respected guest from abroad go through such a degrading encounter.

Police check-post at the Mugrabi gate

At the security check we were told to stand aside while non-Jews and tourists were allowed through with their guides, and only when all the tourists passed, did the police officers feel free to deal with us. We were asked to empty our pockets, remove our shoes and go though the metal detector doorway. Then we were photographed, our IDs checked, and the information was copied into a notebook. Afterwards, we were given the rundown of the rules regarding our visit to the Mount - don't pray, don't bow, don't tear your shirt in mourning, or do anything else that might cause the Muslims to think you are partaking in an act of Jewish observance. The officer then asked me to translate the rules to Dr. Gelfand. When he felt that we both understood our restrictions, he told us: "Have a nice tour and don't forget; the Mount will be closed to Jews in twenty minutes, so make it quick". While I was used to all this, I felt embarrassment for this guest, a fine American Jew who wasn't yet desensitized to this outrage. Unfortunately it is a feeling I have experienced often, and it is shared by other Temple tour guides, who are concerned for the dignity of their guests.

American journalist Aaron Klein, who took part in a tour of the Temple Mount along with several Christian archeologists, gave the following report:

The small group was warned in advance not to bring Bibles and, once on the Mount, not to whisper or make bowing movements for fear the Waqf might think a non-Muslim is praying in the area. The Temple Mount was reopened to non-Muslims on August 2003. It is still open to Jews, but only Sundays through Thursdays, 7:30 a.m. to 10 a.m. and 12:30 p.m. to 1:30 p.m., and not on any Christian, Jewish, or Muslim holidays or other days considered "sensitive" by the Waqf, the Muslim custodians of the Temple Mount. During "open" days, Jews and Christian are allowed to ascend the Temple Mount, usually through organized tours and only if they conform first to a strict set of guidelines, which include demands that they not pray or bring any "holy objects" to the site. Rules are enforced by Waqf agents, who watch tours closely and alert nearby Israeli police to any breaking of their guidelines. 'You also can't bring anything with Hebrew letters, even secular Hebrew books. The Waqf confiscated many of my tour books. One time

I brought a guy who pulled out the Hebrew newspaper, and they took that from him.[26]

It is absurd and obscene that such a blatant violation of freedom of religion takes place in Israel, of all places, precisely on the holiest site of Judaism! According to the dry Israeli law, such discrimination is prohibited:

"Whosoever does anything likely to violate the freedom of access of the members of the different religions to the places sacred to them or their feelings with regard to those places shall be liable to imprisonment for a term of five years."[27]

"The Holy Places shall be protected from desecration and any other violation and from anything likely to violate the freedom of access of

---

[26] Aaron Klein - World Net Daily, February 17, 2005.
[27] Law for the Protection of Holy Places 2.b; June 27, 1967.

the members of the different religions to the places sacred to them or their feelings towards those places."[28]

Yet these above laws are utterly irrelevant when it comes to the Temple Mount. Activists and organizations for the Temple Mount have petitioned the Israeli court system on several occasions, requesting that the court protect their right to pray on the Mount. The court usually finds its way out of acknowledging its own impotence and that of the state, by claiming that the Temple Mount is an ex-territory not officially governed by any country, and the State of Israel is hesitant to take it under its authority.

---

[28] Basic Law: Jerusalem, Capital of Israel; July 30, 1980.

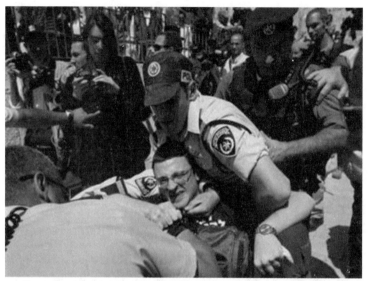

A Jew who tried to pray on the Mount arrested by the Israeli police

Even in cases where the court rules that it **is** permitted for Jews to practice their freedom of religion on the Mount, the police do not enforce the ruling claiming that the "security situation" does not enable them to uphold the court decision. Naturally, this "security situation" is a constant, never changing for the better, and the bottom line is that Jews are prohibited from praying on the Temple Mount, no matter what the court decides!

What emerges from all this is that concerning the Temple Mount, the Israeli government gets its orders from Islamic leaders, who vehemently forbid Jewish prayer on the Temple Mount. One of these leaders who the Israeli authorities acquiesce to is Adnan Al Husseini, head of the Muslem Waqf on the Temple Mount. Al Husseini has warned that Islam will never, under any circumstances, agree to Jews praying on the Temple Mount. In an interview with Voice of Palestine Radio July 1997, Husseini threatened to use violence against Jews if they attempt to pray on the Temple Mount, and blamed specific rabbis who encouraged such attempts.

Similarly, in the weekly Friday sermon delivered at the Al-Aqsa Mosque on the Temple Mount in Jerusalem, Sheikh Ismael Nohaba stated on July 18, 1997: "*Jihad* (Moslem Holy War) *is a commandment which we are obligated to carry out.*

Only when this nation launches a Jihad against the Zionist thieves and the hate-filled settlers, will we fulfill our obligation towards Allah. The Children of Israel were enemies of Islam from the outset and continue, to this day, the fight against it with all the means at their disposal... Our battle against them is a religious war."

Yosef Mendelevich was a prisoner of Zion in the former USSR. He was jailed for many years for teaching Hebrew and trying to exercise his national call to emigrate to Israel. Eventually he was freed and allowed to move to Israel where he became a rabbi. Who would think that what he experienced in Russia would come back to haunt him in his new homeland?

The following is the account of how Yosef Mendelevich was "back in the U.S.S.R."

"*In November, 1994 we went up to the Temple Mount during the holiday of Chanuka to celebrate the historical victory of Yehuda Maccabee there. Our aim was to light a Chanukah candle. I felt that the true meaning of Hanukkah was to be courageous in the struggle for the independence of our country. As Yehuda HaLevi wrote in his eleventh century book, 'The Kuzari', the Temple was the heart of the Jewish nation, and that, 'if the Temple Mount is not in our hands, the heart will be sick'.* "

As Mendelevich's group was walking on the Temple Mount, they were attacked by a mob of Arabs who were yelling and screaming that they were on an Arab site, forbidden to Jewish worshippers. Several Israeli policemen arrived at the site and promptly arrested the Jews and took them to Jerusalem's Central Prison at the Russian Compound. They were questioned for hours and finally brought before a judge who was asked to extend their detention in order to allow the police to continue its investigation of the "crime" of lighting a Chanuka candle on the Temple Mount.

We were fingerprinted and photographed, as if we were criminals. It was all very unpleasant for me, because I had been through all this before with the KGB. We were sure we did the right thing by going up to pray there on Hanukkah and felt very privileged to have done so. We realized we were making a very important contribution to our Jewish People in their struggle to regain control over the Temple Mount.[29]

At least in those days a Jew was allowed to ascend the Mount, but not to pray. But in September, 2000, an event took place which "officially" banned Jews

---

[29] Yosef Mendelevich interview on Ruth Matar's radio show, November 29, 1994.

from the Mount altogether for the next several years. In a political move, just a few months before elections, Ariel Sharon paid the Mount a visit, causing the Arabs to erupt in violence. The Israelis called it "the second Intifada", but the Arabs termed it the "Al-Aqsa War" – for it is the Temple Mount which they regard as the focal point of the conflict in their war with the Jews. In any case, from that day onward, the Mount was hermetically closed off to Jews for three years.

It was to protest this ban which motivated Yisrael Meir Cohen and Michael Kleiner's Herut party to organize a major demonstration in Jerusalem in early August 2002. Starting from the Jaffa Gate, Yisrael led a group of about a thousand people towards the direction of the Temple Mount. After Rabbi Yisrael Ariel and Michael Kleiner addressed the crowd, we proceeded through the Old City, through the Jewish Quarter, and started to make our way down the steps to the Western Wall Plaza. At this point, the Israeli police set up a blockade preventing us from continuing through the Western Wall Plaza, thus denying us access to the gates of the Temple Mount. An intense negotiation process of over an hour escalated into a full-fledged riot between demonstrators and police. Yonatan Hakimi, a demonstrator from Kfar Tapuach was severely beaten by police and dragged away to a nearby police station. The police succumbed to our pressure, and agreed to allow us to enter the Temple Mount from an alternate gate - HaKotel HaKatan. Hundreds of people arrived and started banging on the gate, demanding to enter, but police would not allow it. Eventually, the crowd turned away towards the police station to demand the release of Hakimi.

Waving placards that read 'Free the Temple Mount,' and wearing T-shirts that read 'The Temple Mount is for the Jews, Mecca is for the Arabs,' the largely religious crowd of several hundred made its way through the narrow alleyways of Jerusalem's Old City to the plaza area. 'The Temple Mount, the

Herut march to the Temple Mount in August 2002

holiest site for Judaism, has been decreed Judenrein,' MK Michael Kleiner said. 'This racial discrimination must stop.' Even excluding the religious reasons, the discrimination is amazing,' said 21-year-old Ben Marcus, of Long Island, a participant in the demonstration. 'It just isn't fair that Judaism's holiest site should be closed to Jews,' said Avi Piner, 20, of Brooklyn who is studying at the capital's Mir Yeshiva. 'Anybody who reads the Bible and who knows history knows the significance of this place to the Jewish nation,' said one of the most elderly participants in last night's march, eighty-year-old Rachel Cohen, who came from the Negev.[30]

Only afterwards, when our marathon march was long over, did we learn that the "HAMAS" terrorist group had planned to attack the marching Jewish demonstrators as they were passing though the Jaffa Gate near a highly Arab populated area, but their plans were thwarted due to technical difficulties, thank GOD.

What appeared to be an historic breakthrough concerning Jewish rights on the Temple Mount took place on the eve of the Sukkot holiday 2005. Israel's High Court of Justice handed down an unprecedented ruling officially **permitting Jews to**

---

[30] Jerusalem Post, Aug. 2002.

pray **on the Temple Mount**. Jews both in Israel and abroad were enthused at this new status quo. Now, after nearly forty years of Israeli control, Jews would finally be allowed to both ascend and even to pray on the Temple Mount as their ancestors did thousands of years earlier. What made the news even more welcome was that it came right before Sukkot, which is one of the three "pilgrimage" holidays - when all of the people of Israel are commanded by the Torah to go up to Jerusalem to the Temple. Indeed, the new ruling signified a major change in policy on the part of the Israeli government, police, and legal establishment.

The decision came in response to a petition that *The Temple Mount Faithful* had submitted to the court, requesting to visit the Mount from 9:00 AM to 10:30 AM, instead of the usual 7:30 AM to 9:00 AM. They planned a procession down to the Shiloach Spring in the city of David. There, they planned to hold a ceremony to commemorate the "*nisuch haMiyam*[31] - a ritual that the Kohenim had performed centuries earlier in the Temple during Succot. They planned to collect the pure waters from this spring, and then bring it up to the Temple Mount to pour on the site where the holy altar once stood. The ceremony was also a blessing for rain, and indeed, a few years earlier on Succot, when Rabbi David Cohen managed to enter the Temple Mount dressed in *begdi kehona*[32] and performed this ritual, the following season saw an abundance of rain.

Originally, *The Temple Mount Faithful* requested from the Supreme Court that it be allowed to enter the Temple Mount enclosure between 1:00 and 2:00 PM. When they were refused, they tried again for an earlier time. Imagine their joy and

---

[31] Water libation offered on the alter.
[32] Ritual outfit worn by Kohanim in the Temple.

astonishment when the Supreme Court gave authorization for Jews to not only **ascend** the Temple Mount, but also to **pray** there, between 7:30 and 9:00 in the morning!

Immediately following the Supreme Court decision, excited loyalists of the Mount began phoning their friends to spread the wonderful news. Many did not sleep all that night, reading Psalms and studying Torah to prepare themselves for the sacred occasion. They went to the mikveh[33] to purify themselves in pure waters, making themselves spiritually befitting to stand and pray in the holiest site in the world.

The first group, numbering about thirty people arrived early the next morning in great anticipation. Among its leaders was Baruch Ben Yosef, an

---

[33] Ritual bath.

attorney and strong activist for the Temple Mount cause. They ascended the ramp to the Temple Mount gate awaiting this great historical moment. They arrived at the gate, and when confronted by the police, flashed them the official Supreme Court's decision. The police were shocked. Up to now, their major task was to *prevent* Jews from praying on the Temple Mount, and now they stood face to face with an official document from the highest court in the land contradicting everything they had been ordered to do. They frantically phoned their superiors, asking what they were supposed to do. In fairness to them, these low and mid-ranking policemen were placed in a position that was over their heads, mere foot soldiers receiving contradictory orders, one of those being direct from the Israeli Supreme Court.

In the meantime, other groups of worshipers had arrived at police-blockades at the entrance to the

107

Temple Mount, and similar confusion ensued. The police finally informed them that they had not been aware of the High Court's ruling, and were refusing them entry. Despite being shown the court documents, they stated that "*they don't recognize the ruling*" and basically took it upon themselves to negate the Supreme Court decision. And so, it was business as usual that day, with officers allowing only three groups up at a time, **with no praying allowed**.

Later that day, police and political authorities ran to the Supreme Court to try and clarify the issue. Apparently, the Supreme Court Judge who wrote the decision made a mistake! He inadvertently worded his ruling with the word **"*prayer*"** instead of **"*ascent*."** Perhaps it was simply natural for him to word things as such; perhaps he felt he was in a normal country for a fleeting moment. In any case, Israeli authorities quickly turned to Deputy Chief

Justice Michael Heshin, asking him to replace the word "prayer" with the word "ascent".

Justice Heshin read the claims of both sides – both the police and Temple Faithful lawyer, Naftali Werzberger. The High Court's honor was at stake – could it be that a technicality, an inadvertent slip of the pen, could have such enormous ramifications? Justice Heshin examined the matter carefully and in great detail. The police were interested in swift action, and not a lesson in linguistics. Judge Heshin concluded that a mistake indeed was made, but no bother – as miraculous as it may be that the Supreme Court would make such a mistake, they would make up for it by an even greater miracle: by immediately amending the text of the ruling to read: "*enable Jewish **ascent** on the Temple Mount,*" instead of what was originally written, "*...enable Jewish **prayer** to the Temple Mount.*"

109

These incredible acrobatics of the court are for the sole purpose of not offending the Arabs. Indeed, these occurrences got more attention in the Moslem world than they did in the Israeli press. While mainstream Israeli newspapers had taken little interest in the court's scribal errors, the Arabic language radio station, Al-Jazeera described the Jews as "storming" the Temple Mount after the mistaken decision had been made. They said the court's decision might lead to "dangerous consequences."

I do not know whether the above words refer to the first decision or the "new and improved decision", but one thing was for sure: nobody took notice of the fact that an Israeli court was twisting itself over backwards, working at unprecedented speed (just try getting the Supreme Court to amend a decision so hastily, let alone convene on the Succot holiday) to keep Jews from praying.

"It was clear from the beginning that it had been a mistake," said Yehuda Etzion, a seasoned veteran of many court struggles on this issue. *"We never thought for a moment that they meant to permit us to pray at our holiest site."*

During those Chol haMoed days of Sukkot, after hearing about the court decision to allow Jews to pray on the Mount (I had not yet heard of the "amendments" that had been made afterwards), I invited Dr. Edward and Mrs. Judith Steinberg, an aged couple visiting Israel, to go up together to the Mount. The Steinbergs were very enthusiastic and felt privileged to be able to pray at Judaism's holiest site. But that morning the police set up roadblocks surrounding Jerusalem's Old City. This was to accommodate tens of thousands of Arabs who had gathered into the mosques on the Temple Mount.

Even the Jaffa Gate[34] was closed to Jewish visitors, and we were not allowed through. Apparently, Israeli authorities were concerned that the Arab mob might get bent out of shape at the site of an elderly Jewish couple approaching the Mount. And so, instead of the privilege that Mr. and Mrs. Steinberg might have had to pray on the Mount, they had to settle for the "privilege" of being considered a danger to national security.

---

[34] The Jaffa gate and the Dung gate are basically the only access for Jews to enter into the Old City. All other gates are located in areas with dense Arab population, and most Jews fear passing though them.

CHAPTER SEVEN

REWRITING HISTORY

One of the most dramatic Jewish-Arab confrontations that ever occurred was during the Hasmonian tunnel excavations. The Hasmonean Tunnel is an extension of the Western Wall (Kotel) Tunnel, rediscovered at the north end of the Wall in 1987. This tunnel is an aqueduct which dates back to the Hasmonean kings in the 2nd century BCE, about 100 years before King Herod. About 500 meters of tunnel run in a north-south direction along the Kotel, outside of the Temple Mount. Within it exists a rock-cut channel which is approximately 20 meters in length.

The tunnel was used regularly by the Jewish people until Jerusalem was destroyed by Titus and the Roman Legions in 68 CE. Rediscovered in the mid-1900s by the British explorer Charles Warren, the tunnel is less than a meter wide. For more than 100 years, no one had entered it; it remained forgotten in the depths of the earth, full of mud and water, under houses in the Moslem Quarter of the Old City of Jerusalem.

After Israel's Ministry for Religious Affairs re-excavated the Hasmonian tunnel in 1987, it was connected to the Western Wall tunnel revealing the Western Wall along its entire length.

As the Hasmonean excavations were carrying on, the late Rabbi Yehuda Meir Getz, the rabbi of the Kotel and a great scholar, would pray every morning at sunrise inside the Hasmonian tunnel. He directed his prayer at a point directly opposite *"Even Ha'shtiah*,[35] the foundation stone of the world, upon which the Holy of Holies in the Temple was built upon. Rabbi Getz believed that if he could tunnel eastward, away from the Kotel and towards the Dome of the Rock, he would be able to find the

---

[35] The foundation stone of creation, Talmud (Yoma 53b).

exact location of the Holy of Holies. An underground passage located directly under the Holy of Holies has no prohibitive sanctity, thus enabling one to dig beneath it for the purpose of exploration and study. Rabbi Getz was convinced that there had to be an ancient passageway providing access from the Kotel tunnel, towards the Temple Mount itself.

In the summer of 1983 as the Kotel tunnel diggings were progressing, his hunch was verified. Rabbi Getz leaned on an uncovered extension of the western wall and felt an opening. He immediately ordered workmen present to completely break open the wall. Up until then, all the diggings had been in a northward direction, along the length of the Kotel, but away from the Temple Mount. Rabbi Getz was now ordering to dig eastward, in the direction of the Temple Mount. A huge cistern filled with water was revealed. Under supervision of former Chief Rabbi Shlomo Goren, they drained the cistern and found a further entrance on the far side of the open space. This entrance appeared to have been sealed at a later period than that in which the cistern was originally built. Rabbi Goren theorized that the sealed passage had been an entrance for Kohanim, which was subsequently blocked in a later period. As work continued to reopen this ancient passageway, Arabs on the Mount heard banging from below.

Lowering down a rope ladder, dozens of Arabs descended on the scene. They found that Jewish workmen under Rabbi Getz's supervision had partially broken through the ancient gateway, later dubbed Warren's Gate, between the Kotel tunnel and the inner part of the Temple Mount itself. The Waqf guards soon sent down reinforcements of young Arabs through entrances above to "discourage" the work. A subterranean fist fight ensued between Arabs and Jews and the Arabs began sealing the opening. Rabbi Getz brought in reinforcements from a nearby Yeshiva, and after hours of verbal and physical blows, police finally separated the two sides. At the time it was not clear as to whether or not the Jerusalem police were authorized to intervene in the underground excavation since the jurisdiction of this underground area was unclear. The episode concluded with government officials hastily ordering all "new" openings resealed. And so it remains sealed today, with two meters of steel-reinforced concrete making it impossible for Jews to enter this important archeological and historical find.

Following the episode, Sheikh Muhammad Shakra, director of Al-Aqsa Mosque, stated that the tunnel is *"one of the most*

Sealed Hulda gate on Southern wall

117

venerated holy places of Islam." He added that *"the Israelis have found no indication a temple ever stood there."*

Rabbi Getz's lost battle was just one more example of the ongoing Muslim effort to wipe out all traces of a previous Jewish presence on the Temple Mount. Several years later, in a similar episode, archaeologists discovered the ancient Hulda Gate. The Hulda Gate is located on the southern wall of the Temple Mount, and during the period in which the Temple stood, was the main entrance for the *"oley regel"*.[36] Immediately upon this finding, Waqf officials ordered that this gate, too, be sealed.

The Moslem effort to wipe out findings from Jewish collective memory has been very effective. According to archeologist Dan Rahat, former head of the antiquities department, the concrete and dirt

---

[36] Jews making pilgrimage to the Temple.

used to seal off Hulda Gate buried and destroyed at least two dozen objects of Jewish antiquities. In 1997, the Hulda Gate was sealed and its passageway converted into yet another mosque. This new mosque extends over an area of one and a half acres and has become the largest mosque in Israel, able to accommodate ten thousand people. According to a Waqf worker who participated in the construction of this mosque in 1996, stones with decorations and inscriptions in ancient Hebrew were re-cut to destroy their markings and decorations.

On any other construction site in the country, Israeli law dictates that building projects can be delayed for months or even years in order to preserve any antiquities that might lie below. The law even dictates that if the builder chances upon ancient artifacts, he must finance professional archeological diggings of the findings in order to protect them for research. **Yet, on the site of Temple Mount itself, the Muslim Waqf is permitted to intentionally destroy priceless artifacts from the First and Second Temple periods!** Not only are these artifacts of great religious significance, but their historical value is priceless. What other country would allow its national treasures to be desecrated on a daily basis?

One of the most obscene and blatant Moslem attempts to wipe out Jewish historical and religious connection to the Mount began in November 1999, when the Waqf opened what they dubbed an "emergency exit" to the new aforementioned mosque. Over three days and nights, with the help of bulldozers and 300 dump trucks, this "exit" expanded into a gaping hole, eighteen thousand square feet in size, and up to thirty-six feet deep. In short, the Temple Mount was turned into one gigantic des/construction site. Antiquity authority officials claim that the Waqf sifted through the fill before loading it into dump trucks in order to pilfer whatever valuable items they could find. Truck loads of debris and the artifacts from these lawless excavations were then dumped as rubbish in Azaria and in the Kidron Valley.

During the following days, archeologists arrived at the dumpsite and took samples of pottery from the earth that was placed there. Much of it dated back to the Second Temple Era.

This desecration and destruction wrought by the Waqf and the Israeli Islamic movement on the Temple Mount are politically motivated: their goal is to erase the history of Jewish heritage in Jerusalem and the Temple Mount.

Not only on the Temple Mount do the Muslims attempt to erase our history. Israel has witnessed a similar pattern of defacement of other Jewish holy places by Muslims. On October 7, 2000, after constant attacks

Joseph's Tomb sacked and burned by Muslims

by Palestinian mobs, the holy site of Joseph's Tomb in Shechem was taken over, sacked and burned and then Islamized and converted into a mosque. Five days later, the ancient Shalom Al Yisrael synagogue in Jericho was similarly sacked and burned.

The Arab intent regarding the Mount is the same: to turn the entire thirty-six acre Temple Mount compound into a Muslim site by erasing every memory of its Jewish origin.

As the destruction of the Temple Mount continued unabashed, leading archaeologists called on the Israeli government to stop the illegal excavations on the Mount. Archaeologist Tzachi Tzveig said: *"Israel's press is turning a blind eye to the archaeological damage to the Temple Mount".* Antiquities Authority chief Amir Drori called the Waqf action an *"archaeological crime,"* while the Israel's Attorney-General said that *"the remnants of the history of the Jewish people are being trampled."*

When **Jews** came to the dumping grounds to try and salvage some of the artifacts scattered in the debris, the strong hand of the Israeli law was finally felt. A group of ten people, including an archaeologist, were stopped by the police from examining the mounds of dirt and archaeological remains that the Waqf "created" in the Kidron Valley. Yehuda Etzion, one of the leaders of the group, told Arutz-7 with amazement that he is being accused of "robbing archaeological findings." *This is unbelievable,"* he said. *"The police allowed the Waqf to remove these 100 truckloads of dirt, containing these holy stones that are of primary importance to the Jewish People, and yet we - who are trying to sift through it in order to salvage some of the knowledge that is going down the drain here - are being accused of robbery?!"*

On Dec. 27 1999, a major demonstration was held on Mount Scopus, appropriately looking over the holy site where the wreckage was taking place. Five thousand people gathered in the demonstration against the crime. Organizer, Moshe Feiglin, stated that *"the association that passes though my mind here is of an Israeli Kristallnacht - when the Germans destroyed synagogues and scattered and burnt the holy books of the Jewish people on the streets, the world was aghast - but now, when the Waqf scatters to the dust the very foundation of our national identity and our people, and when we try to save them, the Antiquities Authority tries to stop us. I can simply no longer tolerate this; the struggle will begin here."*

The Israeli public began to demand that the government stop the Muslim construction on the Mount. Urgent letters were sent warning that the Arabs were partaking in a serious act of irreparable vandalism and destruction. Further political pressure was created on the subject, when an open letter to Israeli Prime Minister Ariel Sharon protesting the destruction was signed by numerous highly-respected individuals including former Jerusalem

A tractor removing debris on the eastern side of the Mount

Mayor Teddy Kollek,

125

the mayor at that time, Ehud Olmert, authors Amos Oz and Haim Gouri, and eighty-two members of the Israei Knesset.

Israeli law requiring the preservation of all holy places was so brazenly ignored, that a volunteer group with no political, national, or religious affiliation, made up of well-known Israeli public figures, archeologists, writers and lawyers was formed. "The Committee for the Prevention of the Destruction of Antiquities on the Temple Mount" was founded in January, 2000, and they demanded the following from the Israeli government:

A: Stop the destruction on the Temple Mount.
B: Open the Temple Mount to Israeli and international media.
C: Enable the Antiquities Authority to fulfill its duties and guard the antiquities of the State of Israel.

D: See that the status quo on the Temple Mount is upheld and that all changes be undertaken in a way that does not destroy ancient remains.

A truck evacuating the ancient debris from illegal work

But all efforts were to no avail. In February 2001, an ancient arched structure on the eastern wall of the Temple Mount enclosure was razed by bulldozers in order to further enlarge the "emergency exit" of the new mosque at Solomon's Stables. And northeast of Solomon's Stables, some six thousand square meters of the ancient surface level of the Temple Mount were dug up by tractors, paved, and declared to be open mosques.

Finally, under pressure, Israel government officials declared they would close the gates of the Temple Mount to heavy equipment such as trucks and tractors, and that building materials and construction equipment would be denied entry. In addition, they said that no earth or rubble would be allowed to be removed for dumping. Such a decision should not have been difficult to enforce. After all, there is only one gate in the entire area which is big enough for large vehicles to pass through – Shvatim Gate[37], located on the northeastern corner of the Mount. Nonetheless, building materials and trucks continued to flow in and out of the Temple Mount unabated.

According to Hebrew University archeologist Dr. Eilat Mazar, author of "The Complete Guide to the Temple Mount Excavations," the Waqf continues making major changes in the large underground

---

[37] The Gate of the Tribes.

areas, and we have no way of knowing what they are up to.

Muslim vandalistic activities on the Temple Mount are continuing to cause irreversible damage, to the point that the southern wall of the Temple Mount is beginning to buckle. Someone walking above Solomon's Stables, which is located near the southern wall, is practically in danger of falling through the roof which serves as the floor of the Temple Mount on the south eastern side.

Because of this problem, on December 2002,

A Muslim chasing away Israeli police on the Mount

Jordanians experts were sent in to reconstruct the southern wall that had developed a bulge due to the unsupervised excavations in underground Solomon's Stables. Why *Jordanians* experts? Because the Muslims would not allow Israeli workmen and experts to take part and oversee the repairs.

It is on this part of the Mount that tens of thousands of Muslim worshippers pray in the new underground mosque. Their goal is to turn the entire area of the Temple Mount into one giant mosque, an exclusively Muslim area, by erasing and destroying every archeological remnant that may testify to the historic connection of the Jewish nation.

In an urgent letter dated Jan. 31, 2001 from "*The Committee for the Prevention of Destruction of Antiquities on the Temple Mount*" addressed to Prime Minister of Israel Ariel Sharon, the committee details, stage by stage, the neglect of the Israel government in putting a halt to the destruction. The committee demands that firm action be taken. The following is just a very brief synopsis of their report:

Work done to repair the bulge in the Temple Mount's southern wall

"Re: A repeated call to an immediate halt of all the illegal works and destruction of antiquities that continue on Temple Mount by the Muslim Waqf and the Israeli Muslim movement, and the prevention of it being turned into to a Muslim site exclusively by erasing every sign, remnant and memory of its Jewish past, and the destruction of archeological findings that prove it.

- In spite of all of our attempts and efforts to bring to the attention of the authorities the work being done, the Israeli government shuts its eyes and refuses to see what is being done and refuses to stop it.
- The Attorney General refuses to meet with us just as his predecessor refused, despite the serious breeches of the law and the serious occurrences that are taking place on Temple Mount under the supervision of the Police.
- The Antiquities Authority is prevented from going up to Temple Mount.
- The Municipality of Jerusalem takes no action to prevent the violations on the Temple Mount, and does not utilize its capabilities, even though it is well aware

of all that is transpiring on the Temple
Mount.

- The government of Israel continues to
prevent the gathering and salvaging of
artifacts of the Temple Mount, in order to
remove from themselves the
responsibility of publicizing to the world
the magnitude of the crime and their
inaction to these serious matters.

- Sheikh Rayadh Salah, the leader of these
activities, is the head of the Israeli Muslim
movement and an Israeli citizen. Despite
his severe transgressions of the laws of
the State of Israel and the unprecedented
destruction of antiquities, there is no
ruling authority that examines the legality
of his actions. Sheikh Salah stands behind
the current ambitious project "to clean"
and renovate 37 empty underground
spaces, part of which includes high halls,
each encompassing 100 square meters,
with heights of more than ten meters, by
raising funds and donations throughout

the Arab world to make his grand plan
come to fruition.

- All underground spaces of the Temple
Mount are ancient, some possibly
Canaanite, others from the period of the
first Temple, from the days of the
Hasmoneans and Herod, others served as
ancient gates to the Temple Mount, and
others as purifying baths, or a source to
priests who became impure, and other
similar functions. These underground
spaces present a most important
archeological connection to knowledge of
Temple Mount and to the research of its
origins. It is impossible to imagine that
any kind of work in the cisterns should be
carried out without archeological
supervision.

- We strongly protest the continued
censorship of the press and the right of
the public to know about the Temple
Mount, to allow for free examination by
the national and international media. This

is our obligation as a free and open democratic country as accepted throughout the Western world.

- As months passed, our complaints were proven correct, and the Police and government were forced to admit so, contrary to their original denials. In the year it took for our demands to finally be met – such as the stopping of the activation of the stone cutter - irreversible damage has been caused! During this period, a building and ancient remnants were destroyed before the eyes of the Police who did not intercede, approximately 6,000 square meters were paved, damaging the floor and the antiquities of the area, and approximately 15,000 tons of earth were dug and removed from the Temple Mount without any examination! This earth was saturated with archeological findings, and a vast amount of antiquities and stones were cut.

- We are obligated to learn the lesson and to halt immediately all activities on the Mount which continue to cause destruction and damage, as this letter details - even though the Police continue, until today, to deny all the complaints of this Committee. By the time the Police verify our complaints, the damage will be done, as they try to close the stable gates after the horses already escaped.

- In a petition on this matter to the Supreme Court in March of 2001, we presented the opinions of four premier security experts, among them a former Minister of Internal Security and two former senior officials of the Shin Bet as well as a former advisor on terrorism to two prime ministers. All testified that it is possible to stop the work of the Waqf and the Muslim movement. We heard this from senior personnel in the current security network, who disputed claims by Police concerning security threats on the national level, thereby making it impossible to stop the works of the Waqf. They stressed the need to rely not only on the assessment of the Police in this important and sensitive matter.

- We have no doubt that as this irresponsibility continues, future generations will not understand how, while we still ruled here, sat with arms folded during the destruction of antiquities and the subsequent cover-up of this grave transgression.

- No nation in the world would agree to have the remnants of their past destroyed and lost. No other enlightened, cultured country would allow barbaric vandalism such as is occurring on Temple Mount. No person can remain calm, or come to terms with the irreversible destruction of the antiquities and the violation of the law that occur in a site full of cultural, historic, archeological and universal religious legacy.

- We are calling upon you to rise up and take action to stop immediately and decisively the continuation of the destruction on the Temple Mount, as you promised and obligated yourself before you entered office."

The total anarchy on the Temple Mount teaches the Arabs in Israel that they are above the law. The total lack of law-enforcement on the Mount signals and encourages him to build and loot everywhere **else** in the country, too. And he obliges. Lack of Jewish sovereignty and authority on the Temple Mount, out of fear of the Arab reaction, transmits a message of Jewish weakness to the Arab. Once again, the Temple Mount is the key to the change in this perception. We must turn that key and open the door, before it is too late.

CHAPTER EIGHT

WHAT DO THE RABBIS SAY?

There are many misconceptions concerning the building of the Third Temple and what is permitted on the Temple Mount today. For example, many think that it is forbidden to set foot on the Temple Mount at all. Others rely on allegorical sources to claim that the Third Temple will fall from the heavens, ready and built, dismissing us from any action. An old friend, Zev Adelman, z"l used to joke that perhaps the reason Jews don't walk around on the Temple Mount, is because they are afraid of getting crushed by a flying Third Temple.

But Jewish law isn't learned out from allegoric or midrashic sources. Rather, it is learned from Jewish codifiers. The Rambam writes: "*It is a positive commandment to construct a House of G-d,*

139

prepared for sacrifices to be offered within…as it is written (Exodus 25:8): 'and you will make me a sanctuary.'[38] Concerning walking on the Temple Mount, he writes: "…*it is permitted to bring a dead body onto the Temple Mount, and one who has contracted ritual impurity from a corpse may definitely enter there.*"[39]

The fact is, it is permissible to enter most of the areas on the Temple Mount outside the Temple courtyards and the Holy of Holies. Indeed, Rambam **himself** - in the tradition of the great sages of Israel - ascended to the Temple Mount, in spite of great personal danger, and prayed there. He gives the date as the sixth day of Cheshvan (1165 C.E.) and writes that he was so moved to have *"entered into the great and holy house and prayed there on the sixth of Cheshvan... and I vowed an oath, that I will*

---

[38] Rambam, Laws of the Temple, Chapter 1:1.
[39] Ibid. Chapter 7:15.

always celebrate this day as a personal festival, to be marked by prayer and rejoicing in HASHEM, and by a festive meal."[40]

In light of the Arab effort to obliterate any Jewish presence on the Mount, it is all the more crucial that Jews ascend the Temple Mount regularly. By doing so, they are reclaiming ownership for the entire Jewish People, for their very presence on the Temple Mount constitutes a certain element of ownership. All the more so if **masses** of Jews ascend the Mount - this would certainly be an expression of our desire for Jewish sovereignty on the holiest site.

There is a widespread impression that Jewish law prohibits Jews from visiting the Temple Mount on the grounds that it is a grave sin for a Jew to step

---

[40] Rambam, Letters.

on particular sanctified areas of where the Temple once stood. Indeed, in the days of the Temple, a certain level of holiness had to be attained before a Jew may enter the Temple Mount. Therefore, many rabbis forbid Jews to ascend the Temple Mount because they are not sure of the precise location of these sanctified areas today, and we are all ritually impure.

Leib Schaeffer with Rabbi Chaim Richman and Avi Hyman
on the Temple Mount

In response to the notion that Jews should not enter the Mount today, Rabbi Chaim Richman, director of the Temple Institute's international department, writes:

"Nothing can be further from the truth [that it is prohibited for Jews to ascend the Mount]. *The universally recognized Torah authority, the Rambam himself views it as an aspect of the positive commandment of showing reverence for the Temple, to enter into the* **permitted** *places of the Temple Mount today. No halachic ruling can change this and no rabbi or group of rabbis, no matter how great their stature, have the authority to uproot such a principle.*

Furthermore, closer examination of their decisions reveal a hodgepodge of prejudices and generalizations that are based neither on Torah law, nor on fact. For example, the rabbis are quoted as saying that "over the years we have lost the exact location of the Temple." This is an inaccurate statement. While a number of opinions do differ over the exact location, the picture is far from muddled; **there is a great area upon which one may tread with confidence, far from the sanctified areas, according to all opinions***.*

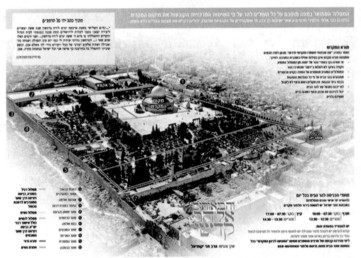

Arial map of the permissable routes on the Temple Mount

The claim that we can not enter the Mount also seems to indicate what can best be described as an unhealthy linkage, newly invented, between so-

144

called concerns for Biblical law and "security concerns." For instance, the rabbi of the Western Wall, Rabbi Rabinowitz, who opposes Jews ascending the Temple Mount, is quoted as saying that "this prohibition of walking on the Temple Mount comes in response to greater numbers of Jews going up to visit the Mount... there is a prohibition against attacking the area... If this (ruling) will influence this, it is a very, very good thing."

What is the meaning of this enigmatic statement? Because of the fact - a blessedly positive development in Israel's history - that Jews are visiting their holiest site in increasing numbers, it became necessary to ban them because "there is a prohibition against attacking the area?!" **Sadly, it seems that there is more involved here than meets the eye, and that political and other considerations may be behind the ban.**"

Similarly, Rav Binyamin Zev Kahane[41] points out that the argument of ascending the Mount or not, is hardly a *halachic* one. In response to a question of why rabbis like **Rav Dov Lior** permit

Rabbi Bunyamin Zev Kahane

visiting the Mount, and others like **Rav Ovadia Yosef** forbid it, Rav Binyamin writes:

*"Someone who wants to get down to the nitty-gritty of this controversy may be surprised to discover that in essence, there is no basic halachic dispute between these two opinions. **No one differs with the fact that there are areas on the Temple Mount which are forbidden to enter, and there are areas on the Temple Mount which are***

---

[41] Author of *The Haggadah of the Jewish Idea* commentary on the Passover Haggadah and *Darka Shel Torah* commentary on Torah.

permitted to enter. But *Rav Ovadia Yosef, who as part of his overall "hashkafa" (outlook) does not consider Jewish sovereignty on the Temple Mount something of burning importance, has no problem making an across the board prohibition as a protective measure to distance people from walking on the Mount's sanctified areas - even if the result is a complete abandonment of the Mount. On the other hand, rabbis who hold the issue of the Temple Mount as something critical; who want to erase the desecration that occurs on the holiest site in Judaism - cannot so easily set up an across the board prohibition, when the halacha doesn't demand such. And indeed, today, anyone who wants to ascend the Mount according to Jewish law can do so, with the guidance of GOD-fearing rabbis who hold an expertise in the subject, and thus avoid the problem mentioned by Rav Ovadia."*

The key is to know the permitted areas where one can walk on the Mount. This term is taken directly from the Rambam:

Even though the Temple is now in ruin ... a person must hold it in awe, as one would regard it when it was standing. [Therefore] **one should only enter a region permitted to enter.** *He should not sit in [the area of] the Temple Courtyard, nor should he act frivolously when standing before the eastern gate, as it is said: (Leviticus 19:30) "You shall observe My Sabbaths and you shall revere My Temple". Just as the observance of the Sabbath applies for eternity, so too, the reverence for the Temple must be eternal, even though it is in ruin.* [42]

All that remains is to know exactly where these "permitted areas" are located. Years ago, I asked my rav, Rabbi Meir Kahane how I can know where it is permissible to walk on the Temple Mount. He

---

[42] Rambam, Laws of the Temple, 7: 7.

told me to speak with Rabbi Yosef Elboim and Rabbi Yisrael Ariel who have researched the issue. He explained that when you have a question in "kashrut"[43] you go and ask a rav who is an expert on kashrut, and when you have a question in "nidda"[44], you seek an expert in "nidda." By the same token, when you want answers about the Temple Mount, you go to the experts.

How unfortunate that regarding everyday commandments, people heed this logical advice, except when it come to the Temple Mount.

To say that there is a Torah prohibition against Jews visiting the Temple Mount is misleading and inaccurate, and does a serious injustice to the many scholarly rabbis who have researched the topic, and who ascend the Mount in strict

---

[43] Jewish dietary laws (Kosher).
[44] The laws of Judaism relating to menstruation.

accordance with all the requirements of Jewish law.

But even without being an expert, there are parts of the Mount we **know** we are allowed to walk on, just by sheer logic. If certain parts of the Mount are forbidden to us due to a special sanctity, there is one sure way we can be certain not to tread on those areas. After all, the Temple Mount, as it stands today, is three times the size it was at the time of the First Temple. This is because the northern and southern parts of the Temple Mount are not part of the original Mount, but were added on later by Herod, during the era of the Second Temple. This means that a large part of the area of the Temple Mount today is no different in its holiness than other areas of Jerusalem, and therefore do not require a special level of ritual purity.

While there are different opinions as to the **exact** historical location of the Temple on the Mount, there is no dispute that the majority of the land mass which constitutes the Temple Mount is "permitted area". When taking into consideration the entire area of the Temple Mount as it stands today, only a small section houses the Temple and its courtyards.

Once we know where we are permitted to enter, that is, which areas are additions and which are parts of the original historic Temple Mount, all that remains, according to Jewish law, is to purify ourselves by immersion in a mikveh[45] or natural spring. This immersion does not purify us from "*toomat met*"[46] but it does purify us from lower levels of ritual impurity. After doing this, we may without any reservation enter the area of the

---

[45] Ritual bath.
[46] A higher level of impurity, derived from contact with the dead.

Temple Mount, as long as we are sure we are not treading over the exact place where the Temple itself stood.

According to many opinions, we are even permitted to enter **the area of the Temple itself,** if it is for the purpose of "**conquest**" – gaining and maintaining control over the Temple Mount. That is, the laws of only entering "permitted places" hold during normal circumstances. However, there are rabbis who rule that these prohibitions may be **nullified in special circumstances**. There are situations mandating that a person enter the holiest of places in the Temple despite the fact that he is neither a Cohen nor ritually pure. For example, our sages tell us that in order to build the Temple, repair, or maintain it, one may enter the restricted areas of the Temple.[47] This is not to say that a person should not purify himself when possible. But if he cannot, it

---

[47] Talmud Eruvin 105a, Rambam, Laws of the Temple, Ch. 7.

should not prevent him from fulfilling other obligations of building the Temple.

There remains little question that this concept of "conquest" applies to the situation today, and grants us halachic permission to enter the holy areas while impure, **for we cannot let the Mount be desecrated and trampled upon by the Muslims in the name of the "holiness of the Mount."** In order to conquer the Temple Mount from the hands of the enemy, the concept of ritual impurity is nullified. The commandment of conquest is incumbent upon every Jew, whether a soldier, a policeman, or a concerned Jew. Every act of removing foreign ownership, possession, and sovereignty over any part of Israel and especially the Temple Mount, is an act of conquest.

Rabbi Shar Yishuv HaKohen, the chief Rabbi of Haifa told me that it is vital for Jews to ascend the

Temple Mount regularly for the sake of "conquest". The rabbi added that ascending the Mount *"overrides the need for ritual purity."* Meaning to say that, it is more important for Jews to ascend than it is to go to a mikveh beforehand, in order to show that the Temple Mount belongs to the Jewish People.

Rabbi Levi Nachmani, also holds that "conquest" overrides all other considerations: *"Since the conquest of Jerusalem, the requirement to build the Temple and to bring sacrifices has been renewed. There is a special requirement of the rabbinate of the generation and the kohanim. Negligence in building the Temple will bring punishment. **The commandment of conquering the Land of Israel overrules Shabbat and therefore annuls the prohibition of ritual impurity.** It is therefore worthy of every man and woman to go up to the Mount to create a constant Jewish presence..."*

If the impression that Jewish law forbids one to walk on the Mount has changed, much of it is in the merit of the hard work of Torah scholars who have dedicated their time to teaching, informing, and clarifying these issues, exploding the myths that exist concerning the Temple Mount. Aliyot to the Mount have become more and more "mainstream", and even distinguished rabbis such as Rabbi Mordechai Eliyahu and Rabbi Goren, both former Chief Rabbis of Israel, have said that Jews can ascend if they know the appropriate areas. The Chief Rabbi of Tel Aviv, Chaim David Halevi wrote:

"The law pertaining to entering the Temple Mount is one of the simplest and clearest. It is known that we are forbidden to make decrees on our own - to forbid the permitted. It is therefore incumbent upon the people in charge to devote their time and energies and make every effort possible to allow and encourage b'nai Yisrael to enter the permitted areas."

And Chief Rabbi of Netanya, David Chaim Shlush wrote: *"It is good to be accustomed to ascend the Temple Mount in our times to the permitted places."*

As stereotypes are being broken, more and more mainstream Yeshivot are ascending the Mount as a result. Along with the increasing halachic clarification of the laws of the Mount, there has been a growing desire by Jews to reclaim the Mount from its occupiers and demonstrate Jewish sovereignty. On Jerusalem Day, June, 2004, three hundred and fifty Jews were counted ascending the Temple Mount. This is an astonishing number, considering that only a few years ago, such a number was close to the amount of Jews who ascend in a **year's** time .

CHAPTER NINE

THE TEMPLE CULTURE

One of the difficult obstacles that stand in the way of rebuilding the Temple and renewing the sacrifices is the fact that most Torah-observant Jews have become accustomed to the post-Temple exile culture that the Jewish people have been forced to live since the destruction. After a 2,000 year exile, we have grown so accustomed to Torah observance without the Temple that we have gotten used to a Judaism that doesn't really need it. We are like a child who has been sent to his room as a punishment, and when finally allowed to leave that room, he doesn't want to come out. **HASHEM** sent us into the exile as a punishment, and now that He has returned us to our land, we refuse to act upon it.

The religious sector of Israeli society has basically stopped yearning for the Temple and for the renewal of the sacrifices. More than 20% of the Five Books of Moses deals exclusively with the Temple and sacrifices (Leviticus and half of Exodus), yet most religious Jews of our time consider the topic irrelevant. Rav Binyamin Kahane asks: *"Do they not understand that building the Temple is not merely one more personal mitzvah, but rather* **the pre-condition for hundreds of mitzvot** *which are dependent upon the Temple?"* That is why the mission before us is to educate religious Jews that Judaism is not Judaism without a Temple. In the days of King David, it is told in the last chapter of Shmuel II, of a plague that killed 70,000 Jews. The sages ask: what sin was committed by the Jewish People to bring about such punishment? *"**They did not demand the Temple** – how much more so for us* [that we must demand the Temple], *for we have seen the*

Temple... [and they did not, for this episode occurred before Solomon's Temple] – Midrash Shmuel

Unfortunately, the subject of the Temple Mount is still taboo in many religious communities. In the summer of 2004 just after Tisha B'Av. I spoke to a Jewish community in Massachusetts as the guest of Reb Leib Schaeffer. After speaking about the horrendous Chilul Hashem that takes place daily on the Temple Mount and the need to show a Jewish presence, the rabbi of the community was so annoyed that I even brought up the subject, he advised members of the community not to support my cause of reviving Jewish national pride and values, because I see reclaiming the Temple Mount as one of them. As Rav. Binyamin Kahane writes: *"Though the Temple is the pre-condition for the appearance of the Divine Presence ("Shecina") even this phrase 'Divine Presence', arouses little*

159

emotion. The truth is, the Torah world has grown accustomed to living without the Temple."

Indeed, the Jewish People (even the religious) have developed a "new" Judaism, detached from what there was two thousand years ago. After living in strange lands under foreign control for so long, we were barely hanging onto what we had. It is hard to adapt to the fact that we are finally back in Israel. And now that we are, we must wake up and renew our heritage, because it is finally in our hands to do so.

Gold and silver vessels ready to be used in the Temple

This is why a growing number of organizations have been established to not only make the Temple a reality, but as a starting point, to make Jews know what they are missing when the Temple isn't built. One of these organizations is "The Temple Institute," which was established by Rabbi Yisrael Ariel in 1985. The Temple Institute prepares for the building of the Temple both physically and in the hearts of Jews. It does so by raising the consciousness of the need and obligation to build the Temple. Over the past twenty years this institute has produced gold and silver vessels according to the Torah specifications, ready to be used in the Temple when it is rebuilt. The production of these vessels actually fulfills part of the commandment of building the Temple in our days, for the Rambam includes the construction of the Temple's vessels as part of the positive commandment to 'construct the Temple.'

Another important movement is "T'nua L'Kinun HaMikdash," - the movement for building the Temple. It is led by Rabbi Yosef Elboim, a chasid Belz, who is helped by his uncle Rabbi David Elboim who actually

Rabbi Yosef Elboim on the Temple Mount

produced "Begdi Kehona," the outfit worn by the kohanim in the Temple. Rabbi Elboim's group promotes Jewish visits to the Mount in full accordance with the halachic requirements. His expertise in all matters regarding the Temple and Temple Mount is unsurpassed, and he lectures throughout Israel encouraging ascents to the Mount. He also publishes a monthly newsletter containing Torah articles and news updates pertaining to the Temple Mount, and which records visits to the Mount for that month.

From the hills of Samaria, at the Yeshiva in settlement of Yitzhar, many initiatives for the Temple Mount have emerged. Rabbi Yossi Pele, Neriya Ofan and others organized a group called "Mishmar HaMikdash" – the Temple Guard. They work to enlist Jews to "stand guard" at the entrance of the Temple Mount as a symbol of respect for its holiness and as a remembrance of the Torah commandment to guard the Temple. The "Mishmar HaMikdash" organizers are also high caliber Torah scholars, who hold an expertise in the subject of the Temple, and they disseminate informative brochures explaining in detail the holiness of the Temple Mount and the halachic requirements for those who wish to visit it.

Shortly after the Mount was shut off to Jewish visitors following Arial Sharon's visit in September 2000, the group initiated a monthly march around the Temple Mount on the eve of the beginning of every Hebrew month. This march, called "Sivuv HaSha'arim," - *around the gates* - has evolved into a monthly gathering of thousands of Jews. The procession starts out at the Mugrabi gate at the Western Wall plaza, and is accompanied by musicians, whose playing can be heard throughout the Old City. At each gate of the Temple Mount, the procession comes to a stop prayers are recited for the reopening of the Mount to Jews.

Yehuda Etzion, who has been mentioned numerous times in this book, founded a group called "Chai V'Kaiyam" – "Alive and Kicking" whose members have tried several times to enter the Mount and pray, disregarding the Israeli police and the Muslim Waqf. They are usually arrested, often beaten, and have been served criminal indictments for the official crime of **"praying on the Temple Mount"**. Etzion has also attempted to reenact the Korban Pesach[48] on the 14th day of Nissan, the Passover Holiday.

Another group dealing more with the nationalistic aspects of the Temple Mount is Gershon Solomon's "Temple Mount and Land of Israel Faithful Movement." Established in the mid nineteen eighties, it is one of many groups in Israel today whose goal is the liberation of the Temple Mount from Islamic occupation, and the building of the Third Temple.

The goal of all these groups is not just the physical preparation of the Temple, but the mental preparation – the return to a Temple culture and mindset. In the days of the Temple, the major

---

[48] Paschal sacrifice.

Jewish holidays were practiced in a totally different manner than they are today; they were almost all "Temple-based". Three times a year, for Passover, Shavuot, and Succot, all Jews made a pilgrimage to Jerusalem to be in the vicinity of the Holy Temple. Observance of these holidays barely resembled the manner in which we observe them today. Passover, for example, was highlighted by the "Passover sacrifice"; Succot was highlighted by "simchat bet ha'Shoava" inside the Temple; Yom Kippur's entire content was the *avoda* of the kohen in the Temple. Today, all we have is a "*zacher*" (remembrance) to these key rituals: a "*zacher*" to the Passover sacrifice, a "*zacher*" to the "simchat bet ha'Shoava," etc. In short, our Judaism today is reduced to being a "*zacher*" – far from the real thing.

A Holy Temple in our days would do much more than change the way we practice our Judaism. It is a whole new way of life. Not only would it be our spiritual center, but it would serve as a powerful **economic center** as well. Via the Temple, tremendous amounts of money is turned over as agricultural produce such as plants, spices, wine, woven materials and animals are bought and sold. As an economic center, the Temple also deals with problems of employing workers, strikes, medical insurance, and also puts out tenders for suppliers, transfers money and expensive materials, and employs many means of collecting debts from those who refuse to pay.

Furthermore, the Temple serves as a **political** center. When our Temples stood, its treasury was used not only for the direct purposes for which it was intended - current expenses and renovations of the Temple - but was also indirectly a form of a national saving fund used by the government in times of emergency, and also provided protection services for the general public. Tremendous amounts of treasures were stored in this treasury, and we see that throughout the course of Jewish history, both during the first and second Temples, that the enemies of Israel often attempted to gain control of this treasury, as part of their effort to gain control of Judea. The desire of enemies to rob the Temple treasury performed an important political function, and was the principle catalyst for the revolt of the Hashmonaim and the revolt that took place against Rome during the destruction of the Second Temple. By reviewing the history of the Temple treasury and the constant attempts by foreign kings to pilfer it, sometimes succeeding and sometimes not, one learns the relationship between money and power – **that it is impossible to be both a rich and weak people**. For when the Jewish kingdom lacked the power to defend its treasury from foreign invaders, it was impossible for that kingdom to be rich.

CHAPTER TEN

REVAVA TO THE TEMPLE MOUNT

In 2004, we established The REVAVA Movement to restore Jewish national pride and values in the face of a Jewish establishment both in Israel and abroad, whose exile mentality was causing a decline in Jewish pride and identity. To achieve our goal, we felt no issue could be more poignant than that of the Temple Mount. For it is the Temple Mount which stands at the center of authentic Jewish-Torah culture. It is the most basic symbol of the national awakening created by Jewish return to our land, a return of our people to its intended path. By focusing on this flashpoint issue, by pointing out its being captive to the worst of enemies, we have succeeded in awakening the "Jewish spark" in many Jews by appealing to their national pride. That is why totally secular Jews, strangers whom I've never met, approach me to shake my hand and ask that I continue "fighting for our Temple Mount."

The people instinctively understand the deep significance of the Temple Mount as a focal point in the Arab-Israeli struggle. It is intuitively viewed as the yardstick to measure if we, the Jewish People, are strong or weak. In a sense, it is like the Temple Mount treasury discussed in the previous chapter. When Israel was weak, it was looted. When strong, nobody dare touch it. Today, the Temple Mount holds the "treasure" of our national pride - it serves as its yardstick. Nobody is proud to be part of a nation that doesn't stand up for its own rights, the rights to its most holy site, and one needn't be a religious Jew to feel this way.

A lack of national pride is also one of the main causes of assimilation. Young Jews drift away from a people they perceive to be losers, a people who forfeit a religious-national treasure like the Temple Mount. By the same token, such weakness is what spurs on anti-Semites, who are encouraged by the weak stance of the Jew. The status of Temple Mount is one of the primary sources for these perceptions.

Rabbi Moshe Segal explains this tie between our national honor and the control of the Temple Mount:

"We must heal the sick body which does not want to be free. We must stir our people to desire

171

freedom; we are part of the sick body. When we will have full and real sovereignty over the Temple Mount, our sovereignty over all of the Land of Israel will be different – as, for example, when the heart or brain is healed and the whole body is healthier.

...The Temple Mount is within our grasp, theoretically under Israeli sovereignty, yet we permit foreigners, in this case, our Arab enemy, to tell us where we can walk and where we cannot walk, and that they will not allow us to pray where it offends them. We could be free – yet we insist on remaining slaves. It is a form of Avodah Zara (idol worship) to look to other peoples for recognition. Freedom is not bestowed – it must be taken."

Indeed, the way to redeem the Temple Mount is by taking action. First of all, the status quo of Jews being unwelcome on the Temple Mount must be changed. This can only come about by a grassroots demand to open the Mount to Jewish prayer. But organized lobbying and quiet diplomacy doesn't work, as we have seen over the last 38 years. At one of the meetings we held with the police at the Merchav David, Jerusalem's Old City police station whose officers are responsible for law and order on the Temple Mount, the top officer there, Yoram HaLevy, told me that they are simply carrying out orders given by the government. He said: "if you want a change of policy on the Temple Mount, go rally outside of the Knesset and speak with government officials". Certainly, he was just trying to push the problem off his court. But the fact remains, that without

REVAVA to Temple Mount posters

reaching high ranking Israeli officials, without trying to force them to at least address the issues, it is kind of pointless blaming the police or even the Arab Waqf.

That is why in the fall of 2004, me and Yisrael Meir Cohen decided to break this policy of quiet diplomacy regarding the Mount – a policy that was getting us nowhere, despite valiant efforts from the many Temple Mount organizations on the ground.

Yisrael had attended an intensive course for Temple Mount guides held by the "El Har haMor" foundation. The objective of the course was to educate more instructors to lead groups on the Temple Mount in full accordance with the halachic requirements. At these meetings, Yisrael not only learned the history and halacha regarding the Mount, but the practical difficulties involved in bringing large numbers of Jews there.

We decided it was not enough bringing up a few Jews a week to the Mount as we had been doing. Something bigger had to be done. Yisrael started pushing for REVAVA to sponsor a major ascent to the Temple Mount by Jews, according to the

Shifra and Ralph Hoffman trying to get though police barrier

halachic requirements. The idea was to have the largest "aliyah" to the Temple Mount in 2,000 years. Advertisements were taken out in newspapers and our newsletter. The campaign was called "REVAVA to the Temple Mount" ("revava" is also a Hebrew word for the number 10,000) We started negotiating with the police to allow a large gathering of Jews on the Mount.

I was skeptical at first, and then surprised by their willingness to discuss our plans. We had hoped to receive their permission to allow up to fifteen groups of between one hundred and two hundred fifty people at a time. We also asked that the northern gate, Shaar HaShevatim, be open to four groups of women who would ascend the northern area in accordance with the ruling of some rabbis.

What followed was a chain reaction of events that went wildly out of control. The police quickly informed the Arab Waqf of the goings on, and reassured them that they were not allowing our event. But the Waqf did not believe them, and called upon the Islamic Movement to take action. The Islamic Movement announced to the press that they would bring out thousands of Israeli Arabs to "protect" the Mount from the Jews. And so, with no help from us, but solely through the dynamic of these three bodies (the police, Waqf, and Islamic Movement), "Revava to the Temple Mount" became an international issue. We were pleased, because as this international "crisis" was discussed, it called to public attention the unacceptable situation on the Mount and its discrimination against Jewish worshippers.

The hysteria that the "REVAVA to the Temple Mount" campaign triggered can be seen in the story written in the Arab newspaper, "Al Jezeera's Firas Al-Atraqchi", a month before the planned event:

Palestinian officials have warned that a massive march planned by a Jewish group to the al-Aqsa Noble Sanctuary will spark conflict. The Noble Sanctuary – or al-Haram al-Sharif - the compound housing the al-Aqsa Mosque, also contains the Dome of the Rock, and is referred to by Jews as the Temple Mount. Ha'Ivri, Chairman of the REVAVA organization planning the April 10th march, is hoping to pressure the Israeli government to transfer full control of the compound from Muslim to Jewish hands. The compound, which is considered holy to both Muslims and Jews, is currently administered by the al-Waqf Muslim authority.

As time passed, the police become more and more nervous and on March 22, less than three weeks before the event was to take place, they issued a public announcement that the event was cancelled.

We countered the police statement with an announcement that the event is on, and we are still trying to work out an agreement with the police. In the meantime, we were pleased that as the event received more and more media exposure (due of course, to the "volatile" situation) the issue of discrimination against Jews on the Mount was getting exposure. This article, on March 22, 2005, by Aaron Klein of the World Net Daily illustrates this:

Police here decided today to ban a grassroots Jewish organization from bringing ten thousand Jews to the heavily restricted Temple Mount to spark an Israeli dialogue about reclaiming the holy site from its Islamic custodians, while the city police department told World Net Daily the Israeli government would allow a similar group of Muslims to enter. "We will not let so many Jews up at once. This is not the usual custom for the Temple Mount. We have to ensure that every Jewish group is going up in safety and will go up quietly," Shmulik Ben Ruby, Jerusalem police spokesman, told World Net Daily.

The police currently allow no more than thirty to fifty **non-Muslims** *to ascend the Temple Mount at a time, who must apply on the day of the scheduled*

Jerusalem Police dragging away a Jewish worshiper
who wished to pray on the Temple Mount

gathering. "We would and we do allow ten thousand Palestinians to go up to the mosques to pray", he said. He recognized Jews cannot pray on the Mount: "Yes, those are the restrictions." David Ha'Ivri, director of REVAVA, told World Net Daily his group's visit will go ahead as planned in spite of police statements to the contrary. "We are still in negotiations with the police, asking them to open up the Mount to more people for longer periods of time," he said.

"We advertised our trip all over the country and have been getting an enormous response. We will exercise our rights as Jews to go to our holiest site.'" Ha'lvri says Israel doesn't have a law forbidding large numbers of Jews from ascending the Mount. "They talk only about letting up small groups," he said. "Show me the law. Show me what legally bars us from going up. There is no law. It's all rhetoric..." World Net Daily has learned Palestinians have plastered mosques throughout the Temple Mount area with signs warning of REVAVA's gathering. Ha'lvri, whose photo is featured prominently on most of the posters, said, "The Palestinians will have to become used to the situation that this is a Jewish State and we have a right to visit the Temple Mount."

Arabic bumper stickers calling to
keep Jews off of the Temple Mount

On Tuesday afternoon, five days before the event, I
got a phone call from someone who introduced
himself as Yosi, a detective from the Merchav
David, Jerusalem's Old City police station. He said
that the Chief of Police there would like me to
attend an urgent meeting and I should come right
away. I told Yosi that I would be honored to meet

רבבה להר הבית
תפילה לשלום ארץ ישראל
03-9060875 א' בניסן תשס"ה

A supporter with canvas sign that reads REVAVA to the Temple Mount

them, but, because it was already late afternoon, perhaps we can meet tomorrow morning. He said that they not were willing to wait until the next morning, and that I should make it over there as soon as possible. Being curious and respectful of men of the law, I agreed. I started out for Jerusalem from my home in Kfar Tapuach.

As I was on my way, Yosi called again and said that the meeting had been called off because they (the police) had decided to **forcibly** prevent our event on Sunday. Their decision was written up in the newspaper that morning:

On Wednesday, police had announced they would close the Temple Mount to Jews on Sunday, the day a right-wing extremist group called REVAVA *planned to hold a mass rally on the site. Police fear the activists could clash with Muslim worshippers.*
Public Security Minister Gideon Ezra and Police Commissioner Moshe Karadi approved an operational plan drafted by Israel Police, which is meant to prevent REVAVA *activists from holding the event. Police will prevent Jews from ascending to the Mount Sunday, and they will work to prevent any friction between Jews and Muslims in the Old City's alleys. Jerusalem police chief, Ilan Franco, announced several days ago that* REVAVA *activists would not be allowed to enter the Temple Mount compound. (April 6, 2005, Ha'aretz)*

184

I told Yosi that I was now disappointed, because I had been looking forward to meeting him to discuss and coordinate our plans for Sunday. We expected many people to show up, and now it was too late to notify them that the event will not take place. Yosi said that he would check and get back to me. Five minutes later Yosi called again and told me to come to a meeting tomorrow at 9:30 with Yisrael Cohen at the office of Yoram HaLevy, the chief of the Old City police.

The next morning at 9:30 sharp, I met Yisrael and Yosi, who was the chief detective of the Old City Police Station, at the entrance to Yoram HaLevy's office. Also present was Effi Havivyan, chief of the Jerusalem police riot squad. Later, Avi Bitton, the Temple Mount police chief joined the meeting. I knew that all these top brass officials were quite busy with their every day responsibilities, but classified this meeting as a top priority. Yoram

HaLevy told us that because of intelligence that they have collected about the intensity of Arab protest, they decided to forcibly ban our event out of fear of Arab riots. He requested that since the Mount will be closed to Jews, we make a public statement and place advertisements in the newspapers informing people not to come out on Sunday. I told them that it was too late to notify all the people who planned to come from locations around the country, and that I would like the police to approve an alternative event at the foot of the Mount, where we could convene to pray and call on the government to change its policy regarding access for Jews to our holy place. The police officers said that they would consider our request, but I knew that they were below the rank where such decisions were made. They suggested some locations nearby where we might be able to assemble, but they could not commit themselves to issuing a permit.

Tension escalated, and the next day's newspaper ran the following story: (April 8, 2005 Ha'aretz):

The police have been put on high alert in expectation of possible violence today or Sunday at the Temple Mount and in the streets of Jerusalem's Old City. The Palestinians may participate in acts of protest and violent counter-demonstrations during prayers, because of the decision by the REVAVA movement to bring thousands of Jews to the site on Sunday, according to a senior intelligence source. "We have very firm intelligence information that the Palestinians view the REVAVA movement's intentions as a threat to the Temple Mount, and they could conduct a violent counter-protest," the source said. "We have tried to take steps over the past few days to soothe the Muslim population, but we haven't been too successful."

The police, in consultation with the Shabak, have decided to bar entry to all Jews to the Temple Mount on Sunday. The warning level about a possible attack by Jewish extremists was raised from seven to eight, out of a maximum of 10. Some three thousand policemen will be deployed in the area of the Temple Mount and the Old City to prevent clashes. Police reinforcements have been sent to the capital from all over the country. REVAVA leader David Ha'Ivri said yesterday that the movement had tried to coordinate the visit with the police. He said the plan was to be accompanied by rabbis and guides so that Jews would not enter areas forbidden to them by halacha. In view of the police refusal to let them enter the site, the protesters will gather below the Mount on Sunday morning "in order to show our demand for freedom of worship by Jews at the site," he said. "We do not plan to clash with the police or to create disorder. I therefore call on the participants to avoid friction. "

While this commotion was going on, I received a call from Orly Benny-Davis, an American businesswoman who is a supporter of the Temple Mount movements. She had spoken with Ya'akov Edri, Israel's Deputy Minister of Internal Security, and convinced him to meet with leaders of REVAVA to try and work out an understanding for Sunday's event. On Friday morning, Aviad Visoly – chairman of the northern branch of "The Land of Israel Faithful", Attorney Amnon Shomron, Attorney Elad Cohen, and I met with Deputy Minister Edri at the public library in his home town Ohr Akiva. The meeting lasted for over an hour, as we discussed our claims that there is need for a change of the status quo on the Mount. Edri said he was stunned over the discrimination against Jews, but stated that he was not in a position to change the decision of

189

the police regarding Sunday's event. It was clear to me, again, that the policy of Israeli officials regarding discrimination on the Temple Mount was to throw the ball in the other's court, for it was only recently that Yoram HaLevy, Chief of the Old City police, said that he was only enforcing the law, and I should speak to political figures.

The point is this: we were able to reach these high-ranking officials to state our claims for the Temple Mount, to place the issue on the public agenda, only because of the commotion and "incitement" our campaign had created. We succeeded in doing what the other Temple Mount organizations could not: spark a world-wide awareness of the Mount, and expose the outrageous discrimination against Jews there. Leaders of these Temple organizations, such as Rav Yosef Elboim, who has sacrificed his entire life for the subject of the Temple, who had seen it all and done it all - was more than ecstatic that the Temple Mount issue was finally getting the attention it deserved.

In the meantime, tension mounted. The Ha'aretz internet edition, on April 9, 2005 reported threats from Lebanon: *"Hezbollah warned Israel on Friday that plans by Jewish extremists to attack Jerusalem's most sensitive holy site would trigger an Arab and Muslim response. Sheik Hassan Nasrallah urged Arab and Muslim peoples and governments to act to stop any possible attack by Jewish extremists on the disputed holy site on Sunday. 'Today, we face a serious threat to the Al-Aqsa Mosque,' Nasrallah told a Hezbollah rally in south Beirut. 'The one billion and four hundred million Muslims must make the Zionist enemy expect that such an attack on the Al-Aqsa Mosque will not remain without response,' he said without elaborating. "*

Obviously, this constant claim that we were planning some kind of attack was ludicrous, but it was used by the police indirectly as justification to bar us. I told them if this is the problem, check us from head to toe as you do anyway. If someone is suspicious, then deny him entry. But why stop all Jews from entering?

Meanwhile, the Islamic Republic News Agency in Tehran reported: "*Extremist Zionists who make up a new group called 'REVAVA,' a Jewish word for 10,000, have stated openly that their goal is to storm the sensitive site in July. REVAVA has said it will march to the site which it calls the Temple Mount with some 10,000 members, aimed at 'reclaiming the holy site from its Muslim custodians'. Israeli President Moshe Katsav has lent weight to the Zionist extremists' bid, calling to allow them to pray at the holy site.*"

What gladdened us was that all the Israeli news reports that rolled in mentioned the Temple Mount as the site of the ancient Temples, as the holiest site in Judaism. After all, the reports had to give background; and this background of the Temple Mount history only served to arouse a dormant nerve in Am Yisrael. It made little difference to us that we were labeled "extremists" and "ultra-nationalists". We were saying simple, normal things that Am Yisrael wanted to hear: that the Temple Mount should be handed back to its Jewish owners.

Three days before the event was supposed to begin, the police presence was already stepped up in and around the Old City. Officials announced that the Temple Mount would be closed to Jews on Sunday and Public Security Minister Gideon Ezra told Israel Radio that the police are on high alert. When interviewed in the media, I said that no provocation is intended, but the Temple Mount is the heart of the nation, the Jewish national symbol and Jews should have a right to pray there, as one would in any democratic country. That's all we're asking, I repeated.

Already on Thursday, April 7, thousands of officers were deployed around the walled sections of the city to deny access to the Mount. More than three thousand five hundred officers set up shop around the Old City, as police reinforcements were dispatched to Jerusalem from all over the country. Checkpoints were erected at entrances to the city, and a large police contingent was already stationed at the Western Wall, with the Jewish entrance to the Temple Mount completely blocked off.

A day before the event, four right-wing Knesset Members - Arieh Eldad, Uri Ariel, Yechiel Hazan and Michael Ratzon announced that they intended to visit the Mount anyway. Following a situation assessment, Internal Security Minister Gideon Ezra and Police Chief Moshe Karadi decided to allow only Muslims above the age of forty and who hold Israeli ID cards onto the Mount on Sunday. The age of Muslim women would not be limited. Meanwhile, Jewish and Christian visitors would be barred from the holy site throughout the day. I accused the police of caving in to Arab threats, and not allowing Jews to exercise their right to freedom of worship. I suggested that just as Moslems over the age of forty are permitted in, so too Jews of that age should be permitted. This request was of course denied. I appealed to the police again to allow us to hold a rally below the entrance to the Temple Mount, near the Western Wall plaza. This, too, was denied. At that point, I stated that if this is the case, I cannot be responsible for what will happen.

In spite of the intense police pressure and official announcements that they will not allow a mass ascent to the Temple Mount, we proceeded normally in our preparations for the historic event. Huge nylon signs were hung up in cities across Israel, thousands of fliers printed and distributed.

The Police were aware of the fact that they could not merely ignore the thousands of people who were to show up demanding to freely exercise their religious right to visit the holiest site to the Jewish People. More problematic for them, is they had no real legal excuse to bar Jews entry. This is why they were resorting to intimidation and threats to have us cancel the event. But we had no intention of canceling anything. The attention encouraged us, and we saw it as a message that we are on the right track.

On Sunday, April 10, 2005, the first of the Hebrew month of Nissan 5765, we made our way to Jerusalem. When we arrived at the Old City, we were met at the gates by a very strong force of Israeli police who had set up road blocks making it physically impossible to enter the walled Old City of Jerusalem, let alone get anywhere near the Temple Mount which is located in the heart of the Old City.

We approached the Jaffa Gate and were stopped by the police. They asked us what our intent was, and we said we were going to pray at the Temple Mount. They promptly escorted us to the police station and detained us for a few hours.

Such was the case that day for every other Jewish looking person who seemed he might be interested in ascending the Mount. It is impossible to estimate how many Jews came that day, because ours was a grassroots effort, and one can't differentiate between a "Revava activist" and a Jew coming to pray at the Kotel. The hysteria of the police even caused them to arrest anyone who looked like a "settler." If someone managed to get through the initial blockades, he was scrutinized again upon entering the Kotel Plaza and expelled or arrested if suspected of coming for the Temple Mount, and not the Kotel.

Also affecting the turnout was the constant, ongoing reports from the police and government that the event was canceled, along with early morning media reports of multiple arrests of REVAVA activists and organizers (Yisrael Meir Cohen was arrested at roughly 6 AM. When I received a call at 7:30AM that Yisrael was already arrested, I knew that it was going to be a long day.) It was even announced on the morning news that any "right wing activist" who attempted to enter the Old City would be immediately arrested - and they made good on the threat. Several buses chartered from cities across Israel from Haifa to Gush Katif were stopped in their tracks.

Jews who got through the blockade gathered near the Western Wall

Only 200 Jewish worshipers were allowed to pass the intense security, which included over 4,000 Israeli police stationed at checkpoints and entrances throughout the Old City, the walled section of Jerusalem that houses the Temple Mount. At the foot of the Mount these Jews sang songs and danced, and chanted slogans about reclaiming the Mount for Jewish worship. Several Israeli Knesset members delivered speeches about the importance of the Temple Mount to Jewish tradition. In the meantime, while the police blocked most of the people we tried to bring, they did allow more than 10,000 Palestinians, including a top Hamas terrorist, to ascend the Mount and hold a rally in the Al Aqsa Mosque, where Muslim leaders vowed violent confrontations with any Jews who ascended the Mount.

The bottom line was that the police reports about the closed-off Mount, as well as the blockades set up around Jerusalem deterred most Jews from showing up. While we may have lost the battle, we won the war of sparking dialogue about the Jewish right to pray on the Temple Mount, making it a topic of debate in the public sphere. For nearly a month the subject of the Temple Mount permeated the media both Israeli and worldwide, and the issue had been firmly put on the agenda. Several members of Knesset showed up at the Mount citing their legal immunity and demanded to be allowed up. When they were refused, they had harsh words for the police and government, especially Minister of Internal Security Gideon Ezra, who was present. Yechiel Chazan, a Likud Knesset member complained that "it's a provocation of the government of Israel not to allow us to exercise our right to go up to the Temple Mount." Even Israeli President Moshe Katzav called for a "solution" to be found in the near future, which would allow Jewish prayer on the Temple Mount in a dignified manner.

We had shown that we are neither "extremists" nor "ultra-nationalists," but plain old Jews who care about the Land of Israel and its holy sites. If that is a provocation, then so is the very fact that we are Jews. We succeeded in reminding the world that the saying: "The Western Wall is Jewish, and the Temple Mount is Arab" is a **false** one, and there is no compromise on this issue. We realized that if the politicians won't respond to this claim, at least the Arabs will, giving the Temple Mount issue legs of its own.

David Ha'Ivri

Bibliogarphy

Goren, Rabbi Shlomo. Sefer Har HaBayit. (Hebrew) Jerusalem: HaEidra, 5758 (1992).

Shargai, Nadav. Har HaMariva. (The Temple Mount Conflict) (Hebrew) Jerusalem: Keter, 1995.

Segal, Hagai. Dear Brothers. (Hebrew) Jerusalem: Keter, 1987.

Segal, Rabbi Moshe. Dor L'dor. (Hebrew) Israel, Ministry of Defence, 1985.

Rambam. Mishneh Torah. Translation by Eliyahu Touger. New York: Maznaim, 1986.

Etzion, Yehuda. Har HaBayit. Jerusalem, 5645.

Kahane, Rabbi Meir. Uncomfortable Questions for Comfortable Jews. New Jersey: Lyle Stuart, 1987.

Index

A

B

C

D

F

G

H

J

K

L

V

W

Y